D0344409

The Art and Science of 360° Feedback

Richard Lepsinger

Anntoinette D. Lucia

The Art and Science of 360° Feedback

Jossey-Bass
Pfeiffer

San Francisco

Copyright © 1997 by Manus.

ISBN: 0–7879–0855–X
Library of Congress Catalog Card Number 96–39195

Library of Congress Cataloging-in-Publication Data

Lepsinger, Richard, date.
   The art and science of 360° feedback
  Richard Lepsinger, Anntoinette D. Lucia.
     p.   cm.
   Includes bibliographical references and index.
   ISBN 0–7879–0855–X
   1. Organizational effectiveness. 2. Feedback (Psychology)
 I. Lucia, Anntoinette D., date. II. Title. III. Title: Art and
 science of three hundred sixty degree feedback.
 HD58.9.L47   1997
 658.4'03—dc21   96–39195

Excerpt from *My Part in a Changing World* by Emmeline Pethick-Lawrence is reprinted by permission of Victor Gollancz Limited.

Quote from Ted Levitt excerpted from *The Executive's Book of Quotations* (Julia Vitullo-Martin and J. Robert Moskin, eds.) is reprinted by permission of Oxford University Press.

Quote from Herb Cohen excerpted from *Good Advice* (Leonard Safir and William Safire, eds.) is reprinted by permission of Random House-Times Books. Copyright ©1982 Times Books.

Printed in the United States of America

Published by

350 Sansome Street, 5th Floor
San Francisco, California 94104–1342
(415) 433–1740; Fax (415) 433–0499
(800) 274–4434; Fax (800) 569–0443

Visit our website at: http://www.pfeiffer.com

Outside of the United States, Pfeiffer products can be purchased from the following Simon & Schuster International Offices:

Prentice Hall
Campus 400
Maylands Avenue
Hemel Hempstead
Hertfordshire HP2 7EZ
United Kingdom
44(0) 1442 881891;
Fax 44(0) 1442 882288

Prentice Hall Professional
Locked Bag 531
Frenchs Forest PO NSW 2086
Australia
61 2 9454 2200; Fax 61 2 9453 0089

Prentice Hall/Pfeiffer
P.O. Box 1636
Randburg 2125
South Africa
27 11 781 0780;
Fax 27 11 781 0781

Simon & Schuster (Asia) Pte Ltd
317 Alexandra Road
#04–01 IKEA Building
Singapore 159965
Asia
65 476 4688; Fax 65 378 0370

Printing 10 9 8 7 6 5 4 3 2

Manufactured in the United States of America on Lyons Falls Turin Book. This paper is acid-free and 100 percent totally chlorine-free.

For my father, who believed all things were possible
—R. L.

To Al, and in memory of Mom and Pop,
for their love and inspiration
—A. D. L.

Contents

Preface

We never set out to write a book. Initially, we intended to produce a series of brief articles that would help answer our clients' questions about using 360° feedback technology to address their business issues: How do I go about selecting the best questionnaire for my needs? How can I ensure that we get the most out of a 360° feedback process? We wanted to provide clear, practical guidelines to help practitioners sort through the maze of choices and perspectives they faced. Even when our articles were received with enthusiasm, it did not dawn on us that there was a book to be written on the subject. That realization came about as a result of two unrelated events.

Twice a quarter, Manus conducts a series of educational forums on topics of general interest to human resource professionals and line managers. Each forum focuses on a specific topic such as strategic leadership, working effectively across organizational boundaries, developing competency models, and 360° feedback technology. We began to notice that although attendance was high at all the forums, the highest attendance by far was at those on 360° feedback. During these sessions, we learned a lot about how 360° feedback was being used successfully in a number of organizations. We also learned, however, about the gaps in information and the misunderstandings among both HR professionals and line managers about 360° feedback. Because we had been working with 360° feedback for so many years, and because so much had been written about the subject recently, we were surprised at the number of people who had little or no experience with it. We were also surprised by the number of people using 360° feedback systems who reported frustration and a lack of satisfaction with the process.

The second event was a chance meeting with Larry Alexander, the man who was to became our editor. He initially came to meet with our colleagues, Steve Wall and Shannon Rye Wall, who had just published their book, *The New Strategists: Creating Leaders at All Levels*. Since he was in the office, someone suggested that he chat with us about possible book topics. We didn't think we had any ideas for books we might write, but Larry encouraged us to talk to him about our practice and our ideas on leadership development. During the conversation, he began to focus on our work with 360° feedback, and after ninety minutes he told us there was tremendous potential for a book on the subject.

With Larry's encouragement, we agreed to do some preliminary research on what had already been written on 360° feedback to see if we could find something to say that would meet a need in the marketplace. We were impressed with the academic, research-based publications targeted at the experienced user and the articles published in professional journals that took a focused look at specific aspects of the overall topic. Yet we also discovered, to our surprise (and delight), that there was no single, comprehensive text that could be used as a reference for getting a 360° feedback system up and running and for ensuring that it achieved the desired results. With this information, and our experiences with clients and the attendees of our forums, we saw that we could indeed fill a gap in the existing literature.

We wrote this book with three audiences in mind. The first consists of human resources professionals who are just beginning to look at 360° feedback as a means to address the business needs of their organizations. These are people who have not had much experience using 360° feedback to solve business problems and have many basic questions that require answers if they are going to use the technology successfully.

The second audience consists of line managers who have heard a lot about "this 360° feedback stuff" and want to understand it well enough to determine if it is the right approach for their organization. They also want to be able to have an intelligent conversation with the "experts" who are suggesting that it is. These people need enough information to assess what is required to make the investment in 360° feedback pay off and to determine if the costs are in line with the benefits.

The third group consists of more experienced HR professionals who would like a comprehensive reference work on 360° feedback that makes it easy to access the information they are looking for without having to skim through dozens of magazine and journal articles and textbooks.

We organized the book into two parts, but the tips and guidelines we offer in both parts will be useful whether you are looking at a paper-and-pencil 360° system or one that is on-line. Part One—Preparing to Use 360° Feedback—includes everything you need to know and do to get a multi-source feedback process started. The first two chapters will help you clarify the business need and determine how 360° feedback can help.

Chapter One, The ABCs of 360° Feedback.   As the title implies, this chapter offers basic information, including a definition of 360° feedback and a brief overview of its history and evolution. It also describes how multi-source feedback is being used, and with whom. The chapter ends with a checklist to help you determine if you and your organization are ready to use this technology.

Chapter Two, The Uses of 360° Feedback: A Tool for Strategic Change.   This chapter contains case studies that illustrate how a diverse group of companies has successfully used 360° feedback to address different organizational issues. These issues include achieving business strategy, supporting culture change, fostering individual development, enhancing team effectiveness, and identifying training and selection requirements. At the end of the chapter, we summarize the lessons that these companies and others have learned in the course of their experience with 360° feedback and offer advice on how to implement the process successfully in your organization.

The next three chapters will help you determine the best method for collecting 360° data and for building support for the process among key decision makers.

Chapter Three, The Most Important Decision You Will Make: Choosing a Method for Collecting the Feedback. This chapter discusses and compares the two most common methods for collecting 360° feedback—interviews and questionnaires. A list of the pros and cons of each will help you gauge which approach will work best in your situation. The chapter also provides a detailed look at the factors you need to take into account when selecting a questionnaire and provides guidelines you can use to evaluate the questionnaires you are considering.

Chapter Four, Using Interviews to Augment 360° Feedback. This chapter focuses on the use of interviews alone to collect data or as a supplement to the data provided by a questionnaire. The advantages and disadvantages of the interview method are described in detail, with advice on how to ensure that the process yields the desired results. Guidelines for conducting an effective interview, preparing reports of your findings, and presenting the feedback to recipients are included.

Chapter Five, Creating Champions: Selling the Idea to Others in Your Organization. The last chapter in this section deals with a topic that is not often discussed in the academic or popular press: how to enlist support and commitment for the use of 360° feedback among key stakeholders. We outline a strategic process for achieving this goal, which includes techniques for identifying key stakeholders and their level of support and for overcoming common objections to using 360° feedback.

Part Two—Implementing a 360° Feedback System—includes information you will need to help ensure that the process goes smoothly once you have chosen your approach and that it achieves its intended short- and long-term results.

Chapter Six, Gathering the Feedback: Tips on Administering the 360° Process. This chapter focuses on how to administer a 360° feedback process in a way that increases people's enthusiasm and ensures a high degree of confidence in the results. It is designed to help you avoid the most common pitfalls encountered during this stage by both describing them and offering tips on how to avoid or overcome them. We also describe several effective techniques for increasing recipients' sense of ownership of their feedback.

Chapter Seven, Holding up the Mirror: Presenting the Feedback. The emphasis of this chapter is on what you can do to ensure that people get the most out of the 360° feedback experience. It describes and compares three methods for delivering the feedback—group workshops, one-on-one meetings, and self-study—and provides criteria for assessing the appropriateness of each method for your situation and audience. Two types of group work sessions are also described in depth—one that focuses on making participants aware of their development needs and one that also provides an opportunity for skill development. The importance of the coach-facilitator is stressed, with advice on how to choose a coach who will best meet the needs of your target population.

Chapter Eight, Creating Lasting Change: Follow-up Activities. In this chapter, we review what needs to be done after the feedback is collected and reviewed to ensure that recipients absorb the messages they have been given and take appropriate action. We describe several techniques that can be used for follow-up, specific strategies for change, and suggestions for making the development plan a document that drives real learning and change, not just a paper-and-pencil exercise.

Chapter Nine, Enhancing Performance Management Systems. The most frequently asked question we hear is, How can 360° feedback be used with our HR management systems? In this chapter, we discuss the benefits and obstacles to using 360° feedback in development, appraisal, and compensation systems. Recommendations are provided, along with a list of what is required to make 360° feedback a value-added part of each system.

Acknowledgments

Writing this book was a lot like preparing to implement a 360° feedback process. It required planning, research, making choices, and engaging in activities that were filled with challenge. The best part, by far, was learning from others and using their feedback to help us test our thinking, shape our message, and present our ideas.

We are grateful to many people for their help and support during the writing of this book. In particular, we would like to thank:

Our clients, including those not specifically cited in the text, who willingly provided examples of their experiences with 360° feedback.

Steve Wall and Shannon Rye Wall, who offered coaching and inspiration and helped us understand why this was an important book to write.

The practitioners, professional associates, and feedback recipients whose contributions ranged from a patient critique of our initial ideas to a detailed description of their personal trials and tribulations with 360° feedback.

The reviewers who took the time to read our rough drafts and give us tremendously useful feedback: Joan Caruso, Penny Nieroth, Harold Scharlatt, and Randall White. Very special thanks go to David DeVries, Mary Eckenrod, Gail Howard, Ellen Van Velsor, and Gary Yukl, who took the extra time to provide a highly detailed critique of an early draft.

Our colleagues at Manus, for their camaraderie and assistance on this project and on many of our other projects that were affected by this work: Marie Boccuzzi, Erik Campbell, Howard Cohen, Janet Castricum, Shay Dvoretzky, Debbie Horne, Jennifer Jordan, Dane Koepke, Anna Ongpin, Bernie Rosenbaum, Laurie Tubbs, Thaddeus Ward, and Abigail Wisniewski.

Evelyn Toynton, whose patience and talent during the editing process enabled us to produce a clear and easy-to-read book that made our ideas readily accessible to the reader.

Our friends and family members, for their interest and encouragement. In particular, we would like to thank our spouses,

Bonnie Uslianer and Allyn Keiser, for their patience and support through many late nights and disrupted weekends, as we attempted to meet our deadlines.

Finally, we thank you, the reader, for choosing this book as a resource for yourself and your organization. We hope you enjoy reading it as much as we enjoyed writing it.

February 1997   RICHARD LEPSINGER
Stamford, Connecticut   ANNTOINETTE D. (TONI) LUCIA

The Authors

Richard Lepsinger is a managing partner of Manus. He is the coauthor of two validated 360° feedback instruments—Compass and Matrix—and has custom-designed numerous instruments to enhance organizational effectiveness and address specific business objectives. His experience includes using 360° feedback technology to help people leverage their strengths and identify areas for professional growth, building competency models to identify key factors for on-the-job success, and formulating and implementing strategic plans to meet organizational goals. A consultant for more than twenty years, Rick has worked with such companies as KPMG Peat Marwick, The Prudential, Bayer Pharmaceuticals, Northwestern Mutual Life, Union Carbide Corporation, The Tennessee Valley Authority, and the Coca-Cola Company.

Anntoinette D. (Toni) Lucia is a managing partner of Manus, a consulting firm based in Stamford, Connecticut that specializes in managing strategy and leading people. She is the coauthor of two validated 360° feedback instruments—Compass and Matrix—and has custom-designed numerous instruments to enhance organizational effectiveness and address specific business objectives. Toni also specializes in one-on-one coaching, facilitating organizational change, developing senior management teams, and designing, conducting, and evaluating strategic leadership programs. Over a twenty-year span, she has worked with companies that include Chase Manhattan Bank, General Electric, The Geon Company,

Household International, PaineWebber, Inc., MCI, Subaru of America, and the New York Stock Exchange.

For additional information about 360° feedback and Manus' other products and services, please contact the authors at Manus, 100 Prospect Street, South Tower, Stamford CT 06901; telephone (800) 445–0942; fax (203) 326–3890.

Part One

Preparing to Use 360° Feedback

Chapter One

The ABCs of 360° Feedback

O would some power the giftie gie us
To see ourselves as others see us!
It would from many a blunder free us,
And foolish notion.

—Robbie Burns

"360 [Degree] Feedback Can Change Your Life," proclaimed a recent headline in *Fortune*.[1] A similar view was expressed in *Business Week*, which cited executives' belief that such feedback "boosts self-confidence, helps managers put more balance into their lives, and teaches them to become more effective at work and at home."[2] According to a study of consulting firms and distributors of multi-source feedback instruments, "Every Fortune 500 firm is either doing it or thinking about it."[3]

What is it about 360° feedback that arouses such enthusiasm in America's top organizations? The quotation at the beginning of this chapter suggests an answer: 360° feedback offers a unique opportunity for managers to find out how their bosses, their colleagues, their direct reports, their fellow team members, their internal and external customers, and their suppliers perceive their behavior. In so doing, it can "from many a blunder free us" by providing a reality check.

Why This Book?

In our role as consultants, we have done in-depth research in the field of 360° feedback for over twenty years. During that time, we developed two questionnaires that measure leadership competencies and influencing skills; we designed customized 360° instruments for a broad spectrum of clients and managed and administered 360° feedback processes for such organizations as Coca-Cola, Bayer, the New York Stock Exchange, and GE Capital. Our work has taught us a great deal about helping people achieve individual and organizational growth through the effective use of 360° feedback. This book is our way of sharing what we have learned, so you can make the best decisions about your own use of this important tool.

We have focused on answering the questions heard most often from the human resource people, line managers, and participants involved in the process: How do I know if 360° feedback is the right tool to address my business's needs? Where do I start if I want to use 360° feedback in my organization? Will a 360° process purchased from a supplier get at the unique nature of my organization, or should I develop a system in-house? How can I get people's support for the process? How can I ensure that the feedback will be kept confidential? What is the best way to keep the process alive?

How 360° Savvy Are You?

Although articles describing the potential benefits or pitfalls of using 360° feedback have appeared in countless business and professional journals recently, many people are still unclear about what it is and how it can be used most effectively. As part of our preparation for a speech to the New York Metro Chapter of the Society of Human Resource Managers, we asked its members, "What best describes your company's use of 360° (multi-rater) feedback?" While 21 percent reported some experience working with 360° feedback, almost an equal number did not even know what it was.

Before we move into a discussion of the ABCs of 360° feedback, take a moment to assess your own know-how on the subject. How prepared would you be to talk about this kind of feedback with your boss or colleagues so that an informed decision could be made about using it in your organization?

The questions that follow are ones you should be able to answer in some depth if you are going to become an advocate for 360° feedback. Read them over, and ask yourself how confident you are of your ability to discuss these issues persuasively.

1. What is 360° feedback? How would you define it?
2. What benefits would the organization and individuals realize from this process?
3. What kind of information is collected about people in the 360° feedback process? What are the different ways to collect 360° feedback? Which would you recommend?
4. For which organizational levels in your company is 360° feedback appropriate? Will people be required to participate? How can you allay their anxieties?
5. What methods can be used to present people with the feedback that has been gathered and to help them interpret the data? Which method would you recommend?
6. How can you ensure that people will take action on the feedback they have received and that ongoing progress is made?
7. How would you roll out a 360° process?
8. What resources do you need to make the effort a success?
9. What are the possible pitfalls involved, and how might you avoid them?

If you feel you can answer most of these questions without difficulty, you have a good working knowledge of the topic and are ready to begin your campaign for the use of a 360° feedback process in your organization. (You will probably want to read selected chapters to confirm your thinking about certain areas.) If you feel you need to broaden and deepen your understanding of the issues before you can be a truly effective advocate, you should probably read this book in its entirety. And if you can give only sketchy answers, or none at all, to some of the questions, relax. We are here to launch you on your journey toward becoming 360° savvy.

What Is 360° Feedback?

The feedback process we discuss in this book involves collecting perceptions about a person's behavior and the impact of that behavior from the person's boss or bosses, direct reports, colleagues, fellow members of project teams, internal and external customers, and suppliers.

Other names for 360° feedback are multi-rater feedback, multi-source feedback, full-circle appraisal, and group performance review. The term "360° feedback" has come to be synonymous with feedback from multiple sources, even though the data may not be gathered from every possible source. We will use the terms 360° feedback and multi-source feedback interchangeably throughout.

A Short History of Feedback

There is nothing new, of course, about people getting feedback on their behavior and productivity. Initially, however, this feedback came from the individual's supervisor or the owner of the business. Descriptions of working conditions at the turn of the century indicate that it was not unusual for feedback to be focused primarily on productivity and to be given at the whim of the boss and, more likely, only when things were not going well.

In the early 1950s, two ideas helped shape both the content of the feedback that people received and the way in which it was given. The wide acceptance and application of management by objectives helped to formalize and focus the feedback process. Bosses and workers were now able to establish and work toward specific productivity targets. At about the same time, research on employee motivation revealed that both productivity and job satisfaction increased when people received information regularly on how close they were to performance targets and what exactly they were doing that kept them on or off track. Consequently, periodic performance review meetings between individuals and their bosses became the norm.

Such "downward feedback," while a valuable tool for monitoring performance and clarifying the behaviors that were contributing to a certain level of productivity, provided only one perspective and was necessarily limited. Furthermore, research has shown that a boss's evaluation may depend more on unit performance than on observations of the individual employee's behavior. In addition, if not handled effectively, or if the boss and direct report disagree about results and the cause of poor performance, these discussions can have a negative effect on employee motivation.

During the mid-1960s and early 1970s, academics and practitioners began exploring the question of how to provide people with a broader and more accurate picture of their performance. Researchers began to investigate the effect of feedback from direct reports—those most directly affected by the boss's behavior—on managerial performance. Several studies substantiated the hypothesis that the perceptions of direct reports about a boss's behavior were accurate and had a positive impact, once the manager learned how others perceived him or her. For that reason, companies like IBM have been incorporating feedback from direct reports into their performance discussions for more than thirty years.

In the mid-1980s, a study was conducted by the Center for Creative Leadership—a not-for-profit research and training organization in Greensboro, North Carolina—and the researchers' conclusions about management development are described in two books. One was written by Morgan W. McCall, Jr., Michael M. Lombardo, and Ann M. Morrison and entitled, *The Lessons of Experience: How Successful Executives Develop on the Job.*[4] The other— *Key Events in Executives' Lives*—is by Morgan W. McCall, Jr., Esther Lindsey, and Virginia Homes.[5] These books helped get the idea of upward feedback into the mainstream.

Says Randall White, who was at the Center for Creative Leadership for fourteen years, "The work we were doing at the Center on the development of senior executives made it clear to us that people's assessment of an individual varied depending on whether they were a boss, a peer, a direct report, or a customer. Our research also showed that people learned from experience—the events in their lives served as a classroom."[6]

Three key findings of the study focused people's attention on the value of 360° feedback. The first was that feedback is an important element of a person's professional and personal development. The second finding showed that the most effective executives were learners—they made everything into a learning experience. The third finding was that many people in organizations operated in feedback-poor environments.

In the case of middle and senior managers in particular, it was recognized that they often received very little feedback on their day-to-day performance; in many cases, they were evaluated in terms of financial results alone. Their personal development needs were seldom, if ever, addressed. But in the 1990s, two trends once again contributed to recognizing the importance of 360° feedback—increasing competition and the renewed focus on the customer.

The traditional hierarchical structure of most organizations had always made for a cumbersome approval process and limited sharing of information. As organizations attempted to succeed in an increasingly competitive environment and meet the expectations of a better informed and more demanding customer base, these weaknesses made it difficult to take advantage of new opportunities and respond quickly to changes in the marketplace. Therefore, many companies began evolving toward flatter structures that required communication and teamwork across organizational boundaries and empowered people at lower levels of the organization to make their own decisions. As this evolution progressed, organizational structures that had been designed to ensure that businesses and functions would be self-sufficient were replaced with structures that encouraged interdependence.

The result of these changes, and of the downsizing that has taken place in many companies, has been that managers at all levels often have more people reporting to them than ever before. In many cases, they are also required to work more closely with people in other parts of the organization over whom they have no direct authority but with whom they are expected to achieve results. In such circumstances, they are unlikely to witness an individual's behavior personally for more than a few hours a week, and vice versa. Thus, the traditional forms of feedback, both downward and upward, yield less useful information than before.

Finally, neither upward nor downward feedback includes the perspectives of a significant population—colleagues, members of project teams, other senior managers, and customers—who depend on and are affected by the behavior of a given manager. These people are also in a position to observe a wide range of behaviors that might not be apparent to a direct supervisor or a direct report.

By including colleague feedback, insight can be gained into how the manager behaves in team situations; as teamwork becomes increasingly important for achieving organizational objectives, this information becomes key. Colleague feedback can also give unique insight into the use of influencing behaviors that serve to gain commitment when no direct authority can be exercised. At the same time, colleague feedback helps to foster and encourage teamwork by making employees aware that it is not just the boss's expectations that are significant.

Feedback from customers and others outside the organization can provide yet another valuable perspective, since they are in a position to judge the extent to which an individual's behaviors add value for the company. Their input can also serve to clarify any conflict the manager may be having between responsibility to the company and to the external client. In this way, barriers to responsiveness may be illuminated.

And these factors lead us to 360° feedback. By gathering information from many different people, it provides a complete portrait of behavior on the job—one that looks at people from every angle and every perspective, in their roles as direct reports, team members, managers of both internal and external relationships, and sources of knowledge and expertise. It is like having a full-length portrait, a profile, a close-up shot of the face, and a view from the back all in one.

When feedback from all these sources is presented within a framework that gives people the chance to practice key behaviors and plan for improvement, it can serve as a lever to bring about real, measurable changes in people's behavior. Empirical research, as well as anecdotal evidence, has shown that 360° feedback can lead to improved performance in the areas evaluated.[7] And with the trend toward flatter, leaner organizations making it increasingly urgent that each employee perform effectively, such improvement is of enormous benefit to the organization as well as the individual.

What Kind of Information Is Collected?

A 360° feedback process can be used to gather information on an individual's skills, knowledge, and style. Because there is a lack of consistency about exactly what these terms mean, we have provided working definitions in Exhibit 1.1.

Your decision about which type of information to collect will depend on several factors—the business or leadership problem or opportunity to be addressed, the role and level of the individual who will receive the feedback, and the organization's norms and values regarding what is considered acceptable and appropriate.

Exhibit 1.1. Working Definitions for the Types of Data Collected by 360° Feedback

Skill	Proficiency at performing a task; degree of mastery (for example, ability to think strategically, communicate in writing, delegate work, influence, negotiate, operate a machine)
Knowledge	Familiarity with a subject or discipline (for example, knowledge of an industry or business)
Style	A pattern of characteristics or ways of responding to the external environment (for example, self-confidence, energy level, self-sufficiency, emotional stability)

The most useful questionnaires request feedback about specific behaviors rather than asking for general judgments. For example, instead of asking, "Is this person an inspiring manager?," the questionnaire might ask, "How often does this person present a clear and appealing vision of what can be accomplished with my (the respondent's) cooperation and support?" By phrasing the items in terms directly relating to the person providing the feedback, you avoid asking the respondent to hazard guesses about the manager's behavior toward others. Furthermore, the individual receiving the feedback will get a clear picture of which specific behaviors need to be changed or used more or less often.

Ideally, respondents should have a chance to rate not only how frequently and effectively each behavior is used but also its degree of importance to them. Such information helps the individual receiving the feedback decide which behaviors it is most crucial to focus on when the time comes to map out a development plan.

How Are the Data Collected?

The most common methods for gathering feedback data are questionnaires and one-on-one interviews. Most questionnaires are still of the pen-and-pencil variety, although electronic questionnaires (on disk or online) are becoming more popular, as companies obtain the computer hardware and software and gain the expertise required to use the technology effectively. Let us take a look at how each method works.

Questionnaires. Questionnaires, which generally take the form of a series of multiple-choice questions, ask people to assess an individual's behaviors and actions in certain key areas. Some questionnaires also include open-ended questions that give respondents a chance to make comments or observations on subjects of their own choosing. There are over one hundred questionnaires on the market today, and identifying the one that will get at the things that are most important to you and your organization is no small feat. The questionnaire you choose will depend, in part, on what type of data you want to collect.

Fortunately, there are several resource guides available that provide descriptions of the most widely used instruments. One of the best guides—*Feedback To Managers Volume II: A Review and Comparison of Sixteen Multi-rater Feedback Instruments*—is published by the Center for Creative Leadership. *Feedback to Managers* specifies which questionnaires collect data on job-related skills.

Ideally, if you are using questionnaires, the process of administering them will include these basic steps:

- People are informed about why the data are being collected and how the information will be used.

- People receive a set of questionnaires, including one that they complete about themselves and similar questionnaires to be distributed to others (bosses, direct reports, colleagues, and internal or external customers), with an explanation of what is being done, along with a request for help.

- The completed questionnaires are returned directly to a central location (internal or external) to be processed, and a feedback report is prepared.

- Individuals review their results, often with the guidance of a trained facilitator; they analyze the information and determine what next steps would be most appropriate, based on what they have learned about themselves.

Since questionnaires are the most commonly used method of collecting data for 360° feedback, let us look at how the process works, step by step, in a representative case.

Recently, Lehrer McGovern Bovis, Inc., one of the world's largest construction management firms, included 360° feedback in a management development seminar designed to help participants target areas for growth. Margaret Van Voast, a project manager at Lehrer

McGovern Bovis, was among those who received a letter informing them that they had been selected to participate. The letter also explained that a 360° questionnaire would be used to collect information on her leadership and management effectiveness and that she would receive the results during the program.

Because she had never experienced 360° feedback before, Van Voast was a little nervous. "I think it's normal to have some kind of anxiety about the feedback, and I did. I thought, 'Oh no, people are going to say I'm a jerk.'"[8] But her anxiety was allayed when the human resources people at Bovis clearly explained the purpose of the program, why she had been invited to participate, and how the data would be used.

As Rich Lupi, vice president of human resources at Bovis, explains, "We wanted people to be open to the process. Because of the way we set it up and implemented the program, people bought into it sooner, and there wasn't much resistance. People knew it was part of a management training program geared to high-potential employees. We communicated two points clearly at the outset: first, the program was for their personal and professional growth; and, second, these people are very important to the company, and Bovis feels strongly about them and wants to retain them. Choosing an instrument that had items people saw as related to their jobs helped, too."[9]

Because Bovis had decided not to try developing its own questionnaire, Lupi purchased one from an outside vendor. He chose a questionnaire that would meet the unique needs of this population. "These people, who are mostly construction managers, don't just manage building projects," Lupi says, "they also manage people and clients. They don't just build buildings, they manage relationships and manage the process for clients. They look at themselves as consultants, and there are certain identifiable skills that contribute to their success in this role. So, the questionnaire we used had to include relevant competencies. There were a lot of questionnaires to choose from. The one we selected was the most user friendly—the easiest to administer and one we felt both raters and the people receiving feedback would understand easily."[10]

About a week after learning about the program, Van Voast received a packet of ten questionnaires with a cover letter explaining the logistics of the process. She read the instructions carefully before doing anything and learned that she should complete the self-report version of the questionnaire first. This would take only twenty minutes and would ensure that she understood what type of questions were being asked, so she could decide who could give her the most helpful information on her effectiveness as a leader, manager, and team member.

The self-report required Van Voast to identify how often she used a given practice (usually, to a great extent; sometimes, to a moderate extent; seldom, to a small extent; never, not at all; not applicable). The questionnaire included items like, "I clearly explain what results are expected for a task or project," "I listen carefully to any concerns expressed about my proposals or plans without getting defensive," "I take the initiative in identifying work-related problems that need to be solved," and "I encourage cooperation and teamwork among people who depend on each other to get the work done." Van Voast filled out her questionnaire and returned it, in the envelope provided, to the outside consulting firm compiling the results.

Next, she sent copies of a similar questionnaire to her boss, four colleagues with whom she worked frequently, and four direct reports. Their version asked about the same management practices, while also soliciting recommendations on whether the respondents would like her to use each behavior more often, less often, or the same amount. Included with these questionnaires was a cover letter, provided for her by the company handling the process, explaining that she wanted their feedback about her behavior to help her map out a personal development plan. The letter assured them that their answers would be kept confidential, that is, when she received her feedback report, she would not know who had said what. The people she chose filled out the questionnaire and returned it to the same outside party.

Approximately a month later, Van Voast arrived at the scheduled two-day training program prepared for the worst. The program was facilitated by a consultant employed by the same firm that had developed the questionnaire and produced the feedback reports. After a brief introduction, each person received an individualized feedback report. When the feedback arrived, it proved not to be as devastating as Van Voast had feared. "The nice thing about it," she says, "was that everyone who had completed a questionnaire about me included positive stuff along with the stuff that wasn't so positive. When you hear a lot of good things about yourself, it's easier to say, 'Okay, well, I'm really good at this, but I ought to work on that.'"[11]

After they had spent some time reviewing the feedback on their own, the facilitator asked the participants to form smaller work groups. The small groups then engaged in a series of exercises designed to help them think about their feedback in the context of their actual work environment in order to clarify their key strengths and identify areas in need of further development. As Van Voast reports, "I realized that I sometimes tried too hard to get consensus instead of saying, 'We have to do it this way, and this is what we're going to do.' I realized you can't always have democratic rule and get the job done. Sometimes, the team wants you to make the call. While it's good to get other people's input on decisions, there is such a thing as too much information."[12]

One-on-one Interviews. Ideally, if you are using individual interviews, the process will include these basic steps:

- As with the questionnaire process, the feedback recipient is informed about why the data are being collected and how they will be used.
- The feedback recipient helps determine what questions will be asked and who will be interviewed.

- The interviewer schedules and conducts the one-on-one interviews.
- The interviewer prepares a summary report that includes the key themes and patterns, with representative (but anonymous) quotes about the person's behavior.
- The feedback recipient and the individual who collected the data and prepared the report meet to review the findings and discuss the next steps.
- The recipient creates a personal development plan that involves specific activities, target dates, and progress review points.

Individual interviews can serve as a stand-alone method of data collection or as a complement to the data collected by questionnaires. The interviews can be conducted at the same time the questionnaire is administered or as a follow-up activity to elaborate on or clarify the findings provided by the questionnaire. For example, having received questionnaire feedback from her boss, selected direct reports, and colleagues, Diane Frimmel, senior vice president and director of operations at PaineWebber, decided to use interviews to better understand the messages she had received. She also used the interview data to fine-tune her development plan and determine how to gain the support of others as she set out to achieve her leadership and management goals. From Frimmel's perspective, "The questionnaire data were very useful but raised as many questions as they answered for me." She went on to explain, "If I were going to take a next step based on these data and use it for professional development, I needed to get more specific information about the critical messages that were raised in the questionnaire. The interviews allowed me to clarify information I felt was essential."[13]

Many practitioners believe that multiple data collection methods provide the best picture of an individual's behavior. One proponent of this approach is David DeVries, formerly an executive vice president of the Center for Creative Leadership and presently co-president of Kaplan-DeVries, a consulting firm that specializes in using 360° feedback for executive development. DeVries feels that, "feedback should involve different sources and different modes or media. I would argue for the addition of interviews as an integral part of any 360° questionnaire method. When you hand out a questionnaire, you collect a certain kind of data that are helpful but tend to be more global. It's awfully useful to complement that with interviews, which provide a very different kind of data. They don't negate or contradict what is in the questionnaire but offer concrete examples."[14] Randall White agrees: "Interviews provide context, not just strengths and weaknesses. They flesh out the questionnaire data." He adds, "But most organizations don't have the resources to collect that kind of data."[15]

Where Is 360° Feedback Being Used?

Although 360° feedback is used at all levels in today's organizations, its most frequent use is with managerial populations, especially at the more senior levels. The members of the Society of Human Resource Managers who responded to our survey about the use of 360° feedback indicated that their organizations are using 360° feedback primarily for executives and upper-middle managers (35 percent and 37 percent respectively). Twenty-three percent said it is being used with middle managers, 18 percent said they use it with first-level managers, and 11 percent indicated it was being used with individual contributors. Respondents were able to select more than one response, so it is safe to assume that several organizations use the technology with more than one level of their population. (This also explains why the percentages add up to more than 100 percent.)

We asked several heads of human resource functions and managers of training and development how their organizations decided which level of manager should be the first to receive 360° feedback. Marion Jacobson, vice president and director of corporate training at PaineWebber, expressed the views of many of those who had opted to start with senior management when she said, "We chose that route because we wanted to show people at other levels that they were part of senior management's development and also to provide them with a model for being open. When they saw that top-level executives were willing to open up to what people were saying about them and to the fact that they needed to develop their skills, it created more willingness on the part of less senior people to undergo the process later on. And in fact, the anecdotal accounts from the senior people were so fantastic, it made people at other levels much more excited about trying it."[16]

Steve Gonabe, vice president of training and development for Household International, where senior-level executives were also the first to receive 360° feedback, explained that the decision was based on the desire to initiate broad culture change. "We wanted to make sure that people were not only getting results but were behaving in a way that was consistent with the culture that our CEO, Bill Aldinger, was trying to instill in the organization. To bring about real culture change, we felt we needed to start with the most senior people, so that the effects would filter down throughout the company."[17]

How Is 360° Feedback Being Used?

When asked, "How is 360° (multi-rater) feedback being used in your company?," 58 percent of the human resource managers in our survey responded that it was being used for management and organizational development; 25 percent indicated that it was being used for performance appraisal; 20 percent said it was used to support strategy implementation and culture change, and 19 percent cited its use for team development. (Respondents were asked to select all answers that applied, so total responses were greater than 100 percent.) In another study, twenty consulting firms reported that 85 percent of their clients who use multi-source feedback use it for development purposes. Clearly, development appears to be the most frequent application of this feedback technology.[18]

Our own practice supports these findings. We have, however, begun to observe a trend toward a broader use of 360° feedback, as organizations get more comfortable with the technology and become more aware of its potential to facilitate change. Having helped hundreds of companies solve a wide range of business issues, we have seen 360° feedback used effectively in a number of ways in addition to development. What follows is a list of other applications for multi-source feedback that have proved effective.

To achieve business strategy and culture change by clarifying the behaviors that are required to support these initiatives

Once an organization has clarified its strategic direction and determined its business objectives, a 360° feedback process can be a key element in refocusing the workforce to attain changed organizational goals through changing their behavior.

Real culture change can be achieved only by getting people at all levels of the organization to behave in ways that support the change. Leaders will need both to adopt new behaviors and to encourage different kinds of behavior in others. People need to know not only what will be required of them in the future but how much divergence there is between their current behavior and future expectations.

Gathering feedback on the relevant behaviors sends a clear message to people throughout the organization about what is important and what will be evaluated and rewarded. Since the manager's boss, direct reports, and peers are often in the best position to observe his or her current behavior and highlight any gaps relative to expectations, 360° feedback can be a highly effective starting point for change.

To enhance team effectiveness

The behaviors that contribute to an individual's effectiveness as a member of a team are very different from those required in more traditional hierarchical relationships. As organizations increasingly turn to team structures—cross-functional teams of various tenure—to improve profitability through enhanced efficiency, responsiveness, and quality, people find they have to learn a new set of skills. Many companies are developing 360° feedback processes that focus on skills required for effective teamwork; the data they gather can both clarify which behaviors are most essential and help people understand what they have to do to help improve team effectiveness.

As part of human resource management systems, to ensure that critical job-related behaviors are being developed, evaluated, and rewarded

Just as individuals use 360° feedback to determine their own development needs, organizations can use aggregate reports to create a profile of training and development needs across the company. This profile makes it possible to plan effective interventions—training, job assignments, mentoring, or coaching—to improve people's performance or help them align their behavior with organizational goals and values.

Recent trends indicate that the use of multi-source feedback for administrative purposes is on the rise.[19] More and more performance appraisal systems are being revamped to include evaluations from peers and direct reports.[20] Fifty percent of companies that responded to a recent survey indicated that multi-source feedback was being used for formal appraisal, job placement, pay decisions, and downsizing. In fact, one organization that compared the predictive accuracy of its assessment center data and that of direct report feedback discovered that feedback of direct reports was a better predictor of leadership effectiveness.[21]

A detailed example of each of these applications is given in Chapter Two. In most cases, we found that the feedback process addressed more than one of these goals. This is because the goals themselves, as they are defined by the organization, may be intricately entwined. For example, promoting culture change and achieving business objectives are seldom approached as two distinct, separate aims; rather, the culture change itself is generally intended to serve a business purpose.

Key Decisions About Using 360° Feedback

If you decide that 360° feedback can prove useful to your organization, you and your colleagues will have important decisions to make about the levels in the organization where you will use it, the method you will use to collect the data, the questionnaire you will use for the chosen method, and how you will help people understand the feedback and determine next steps. These decisions will vary according to the purpose of the feedback, the nature of your company, and the resources available.

This book focuses on providing you with the information you need to make the best possible decisions about the following:

The right approach for collecting and presenting feedback in your organization

You will need to consider which skills, knowledge, and styles are relevant in order to decide what the focus of the information-gathering process should be—whether you want to gather feedback through questionnaires, one-on-one interviews, or some combination of the two; whether to purchase a questionnaire, if one is to be used, or to develop it in-house; how to find the best questionnaire for your purposes, if the decision is to purchase; and whether to present the feedback in one-on-one meetings or in group settings.

Generating enthusiasm and commitment among key decision makers in the organization

Widespread support is important for getting the green light for a 360° feedback process and for ensuring its ultimate success. In particular, the support of senior managers should be enlisted as early in the process as possible. Such support can best be generated by

linking the 360° process with specific business initiatives and clarifying the cost and benefits to both the organization and individual
employees. When key decision makers understand that the feedback
has a role to play within the context of larger organizational goals,
they are more likely to become advocates for the process. And once
senior managers are committed to the idea, they can communicate
their enthusiasm to those at lower levels of the organization.

Ensuring that the data collected are useful and of high quality

You will want to design the program to increase the likelihood
that participants will receive useful data in a nonthreatening form
and environment. Issues to be addressed include how to protect the
confidentiality of raters, how to select and ensure a sufficient number
of respondents, how to present the feedback in the most effective way
possible, and how to make it clear to participants the ways in which
the feedback can help them increase their job effectiveness.

Providing meaningful training, development, and follow-up activities

You will need to consider what kind of individual counseling
and monitoring should be provided during and after the program,
what sort of training courses will be most useful and how to make
them available, how best to ensure that people formulate relevant,
realistic development goals, and how to monitor participants'
progress toward reaching their goals.

Concluding Remarks

In the case of 360° feedback, both process and content are very important. The way in which the feedback is collected and presented,
as well as the questions asked, can have an enormous effect on how
feedback is received. For that reason, you will want to give careful
consideration to the design of the process, in order to make sure
that it serves the purpose for which it is intended.

Chapter Two

The Uses of 360° Feedback

A Tool for Strategic Change

I find the great thing in this world is not so
much where we stand, as in the direction we are
moving: To reach the port of heaven, we must sail
sometimes with the wind and sometimes against
it—but we must sail, and not drift, nor lie at anchor.

—*Oliver Wendell Holmes*

To decide whether 360° feedback could be useful in your organization, ask yourself the following questions:

- Can your company meet the challenges represented by developments like consolidation, increased competition, global expansion, and deregulation using the same skills and behaviors as in the past?

- If people need to change their behaviors to ensure the organization's future success, are they clear about exactly what they need to do differently, and do they feel equipped to make those changes?

- Is the behavior of people in the organization sufficiently consistent with the vision, mission, and espoused values of the company?

- Is there a formal system in place through which people receive information on how others perceive their behavior and their performance? Has it been structured to relate directly to the skills and practices most important to their jobs?

- Do selection and development systems accurately reflect the current and future requirements of the jobs being done?

You are not alone if you answered "no" to one or more of the above questions. In Chapter One, we briefly mentioned how 360° feedback can be used to help promote culture change, achieve a business strategy, enhance team effectiveness, and identify training and selection requirements. In this chapter, we will introduce you to some of the companies that have used it to attain those ends and will describe the role it played. While we are far from prescribing 360° feedback as the cure-all for every corporate challenge or problem, our work with a broad spectrum of organizations over the last twenty years has convinced us of the range and effectiveness of its potential applications.

Achieving Business Strategy: United Jersey Bank Financial

Like many other banks, UJB Financial went through a series of changes as it responded to the shifts and trends in the industry. In 1993, United Jersey Bank Financial was restructured from six banks serving different geographic areas and having duplicate infrastructures to one company focused on three broad market segments: retail and small business, commercial, and private banking and investment customers. In 1996, UJB Financial merged with Summit Bank and took the Summit name. Upon completion of the merger, the bank will have $22 billion in assets and will serve over one million households throughout New Jersey and Pennsylvania.

At the retail division of what was then still UJB Financial, 360° feedback was one tool used to ensure that individual employees' skills and orientation were realigned to support the organization's emerging business strategy. It was used to translate the idea of "service excellence" and "customer focus" into real and measurable action on the part of every branch-based employee.

The impetus for the program was a 1994 statement by T. Joseph Semrod, chairman and CEO of UJB Financial, that his vision for the organization's future centered on providing "total customer satisfaction." Sabry Joseph Mackoul, head of the retail division, accepted the challenge implicit in this statement. He created a five-year plan for the organization that, as he described it, represented a transition from a "utility" that "appears to agree with the regulators that our most important mission is safety for the bank, not service to our customers" to a "first-class competitive retail organization." Mackoul then decided to help his division prepare for that future by defining what sort of behaviors on the part of managers would help contribute to achieving this goal.

He asked Gail Howard, the senior vice president of human resources at the time, to formulate a plan to refocus the workforce. As one strategy to create broad understanding and support for the effort, she established the retail bank's Professional Excellence Task Force—a group made up of both corporate managers and carefully selected, high-credibility people from the field. The task force began by redefining the five jobs requiring close customer contact: branch manager, assistant branch manager, customer service reps, and tellers and teller supervisors. The goal was to redefine the jobs in the employees' own minds and move away from simply filling orders and administration toward proactive sales and service.

The task force developed broad job outlines for each position. In every case, the outlines focused on how much time should be spent on administration, how much on servicing, how much on selling, and how much on coaching and developing people. From these job outlines, it became clear that the managers' positions required more of a focus on leadership responsibilities, that is, creating an environment within the branches that encouraged total customer satisfaction, and the sales rep and teller positions required more active selling skills, with much less time and attention devoted to reporting and control functions.

Having decided to purchase a questionnaire for the purpose of assessing individual skills and behaviors, the task force chose one that asked for specific information about the frequency with which these practices were used. As Howard says, "We wanted a questionnaire that had a database with normative data to make it more meaningful. We were also purchasing confidentiality—people felt more at ease being honest when they saw the questionnaire was being mailed to an outside party."[1]

The questionnaire was then customized by the task force to reflect the specific characteristics UJB Financial would require of its employees in the future; for instance, a technical mastery section was added to gauge managers' skills with regard to using automated systems and other technology effectively within the sales process.

To identify the leadership and managerial behaviors and skills that were closely associated with the most successful branches, a representative group of eighty branch managers—about one-third of the retail division's total—was then asked to participate in a 360° feedback process that would collect information about their use of these and other significant behaviors. By comparing the findings on the use of these leadership behaviors to objective measures of the various branches' financial performance, that is, growth in loans and deposits, the task force discovered a correlation between profitability and the frequent use of such management practices as informing, clarifying, planning, problem solving, and inspiring. "For the first time that I know of," says Howard, "we established a clear link between managerial competencies and branch performance."[2]

At first, however, there was some resistance to the idea of using 360° feedback at UJB, even from members of the task force. They were worried that the feedback might prove damaging to managers' self-esteem. So Howard suggested to the task force members that they try it out themselves. If they felt it was not worthwhile or that the process would be too risky if broadly applied, some other method would be used.

The task force members embarked on the same 360° feedback process, using the same instrument that other employees would be asked to use. First, they completed a questionnaire on themselves; then the questionnaire was given to their peers, bosses, and direct reports, and they were presented with their personalized feedback reports in a group workshop. Once they had been through the process, they became among the strongest advocates of 360° feedback within the organization. They were also able and willing to speak personally to individuals' fears and questions.

In fact, they persuaded Mackoul and his senior management team to undergo the process, too, and these senior executives likewise became advocates. Howard emphasizes how important it was to have senior management behind her in the effort. "They really took a hands-on approach; their commitment was visible to all our employees, which helped reinforce the message we were sending: that we all needed to change in order to achieve the goals of the business."[3]

It was then time to design a vehicle for presenting the data that had been collected and helping people to analyze and make sense of them. It was emphasized that the purpose of the instrument and the workshop in which the data were presented was to give participants insight into how well prepared they were to assume their future roles in the organization, which would be quite different from their present ones. The program was presented as a way for them to fill any gaps that might exist between current performance and future demands.

In the end, two thousand of the retail division's employees participated in the feedback process. Each one was asked to identify preliminary development targets and to prepare for scheduled one-on-one development meetings with their bosses. During these meetings, they and their bosses reviewed the feedback together and drew up development plans that specified both what the individual's key goals were and when those goals could be expected to be met.

Individuals were given from eighteen to twenty-four months to close their skill gaps. Howard says, "We didn't want to make the mistake that sometimes happens with human resource goals of allowing them to be expressed in vague terms and then not setting any schedule for achieving them. We wanted to send a message that these goals were as important to senior management and the division as a whole as financial goals. Setting target dates says, in effect, 'We take your development seriously.'"

Howard also points out that "an important feature of the message we created was 'It's okay if you don't want to change in the way the organization is asking.' We offered what we jokingly called a 'no-fault divorce'—a rich severance package available to those who felt they were heading for a job that didn't appeal to them any more. So, it was up to them. They were in control. At the same time, we made it clear that the 360° effort was not part of a downsizing, that there was room for everyone who wanted to stay, and we were pleased at how few people took the option to leave."[4]

Based on the composite feedback, the corporate training department set about identifying significant skill gaps in the division and figuring out whether there were internal courses in place to address them. In cases where such programs did not exist, they were either developed internally or located outside the bank, so employees could attend them on their own schedules. Managers also went through a coaching course that emphasized giving constructive feedback and empowering their direct reports.

One of the notable features of the UJB approach was the integration of the behaviors measured by the 360° questionnaire into the performance appraisal system. It was redesigned to reflect the new job descriptions, using the same language as the competency model. The organization also announced that reward systems would be overhauled to reflect people's progress toward achieving their development goals.

As for the resistance that had been anticipated among the managers: it never really materialized. Dan Slocum, a regional manager, expressed what seemed to be the general feeling when he said, "It was the first time in my career I'd ever really learned how my boss and my direct reports saw me. I couldn't believe how helpful it was to get that kind of perspective—it made me understand both my strengths and the areas I had to work on much more clearly. And it wasn't even as painful as I'd expected!"[5]

Supporting Culture Change:
The Landmark Stock Exchange

The Landmark Stock Exchange[6] is one of several stock exchanges in the United States. In the last decade, technological advances and the globalization of financial markets have given rise to a crop of new markets in the United States and around the world. This heightened competitive environment posed a new challenge for Landmark. "Getting to be one of the premiere stock exchanges in the country is a difficult enough task," said Debra S. Samulski, group executive vice president, "and staying there will be even harder."

When Jack Friedman was appointed chairman of the Landmark Stock Exchange, he had a very clear picture of what direction he wanted Landmark to take for the future. In addition to focusing on domestic listings, he wanted to attract overseas companies to list their shares with Landmark. He also wanted to enhance the perception of Landmark as a leader in the use of technology to serve its constituents.

Friedman was very conscious that Landmark was facing unprecedented and intensifying competition for business; as he saw it, Landmark had to be ready to reinvent itself, daily if necessary, to meet the challenges of the future. Only by being the best marketplace in the world, with superior technology in place not only to handle enlarged volumes but to do so in the fastest, most accurate way of any exchange, could it maintain a competitive advantage.

As the drive toward reinventing Landmark gathered momentum, Dave Burns, managing director of human resource planning and development, was also concerned about the degree to which Landmark's vision for the future was understood and being translated into action throughout the organization. Burns was aware that Landmark's espoused values—integrity, excellence, customer commitment, and respect for the individual—had to be practiced consistently across the organization. Without question, integrity had served as the foundation of Landmark's success. In Burns's opinion, the time had come to ensure that excellence, customer commitment, and respect for the individual were not only reflected in day-to-day behavior but were also seen as critical enablers for Landmark's continuing success.

Every year, Landmark's top managers are brought together for an executive development experience. Since the next Executive Program was due to be held right after a reorganization was to be announced, Burns realized it would provide a perfect opportunity to support the drive toward culture change. He therefore designed a four-day program centered on the strategic direction, the vision, and the culture required to attain them successfully. He called the session *Preparing for Tomorrow*.

The focus of the first part of the program was making sure that everyone understood what Landmark would look like when they achieved Friedman's vision and what their individual roles would be in achieving it. To this end, three members of the office of the chairman took part in and opened a dialogue with the program participants.

The next issue to be addressed was making sure that the leadership behavior of the top managers was aligned with and directly supported Landmark's strategy, vision, and values. It was here that 360° feedback played a key role.

Burns and his staff selected a 360° questionnaire from among the many that are available in the marketplace. He worked with the vendor to customize the instrument to create a questionnaire that focused on the core values of integrity, excellence, respect for the individual, and customer commitment. The items on the questionnaire addressed behaviors that supported those values. For example, some of the items related to respect for the individual included, "I give people credit for helpful ideas and suggestions," "I recognize special contributions and important achievements by acknowledging them during a meeting or ceremonial event," "I consult with people to get their reactions and suggestions before making major changes that will affect them," and "I listen carefully to any concerns expressed about my proposals and plans without getting defensive."

At Burns's suggestion, an optional open-ended question— "What else would you like to say to this person to help him or her maintain or improve effectiveness as a leader and a manager?"—was asked at the end of the questionnaire. This gave the respondents a chance to provide more detailed information that the multiple-choice items did not permit. The qualitative input made the questionnaire results that much richer. Says Burns, "Including an open-ended question that allowed respondents to give their comments rather than just numerical answers was the single factor that made for greater acceptance."

Before the program began, the questionnaires were completed by all the managers and by their respective direct reports, colleagues, and bosses. During the program, they received the results of the feedback, first in a composite form and then in an individual, personalized form. The composite data gave them a chance to examine how closely the behavior of the organization's managers as a whole aligned with the strategy, vision, and values. As they looked at the composite data, they discussed the extent to which current behavior in Landmark was contributing to achieving the goals that had been set and where the gaps existed.

Because the aggregate data dealt with the entire group, it was less threatening to individual participants; reviewing it first helped to build acceptance among the people for the idea of receiving feedback. It also enabled the group to discuss leadership strengths and weaknesses at an organizational level in an open and constructive manner, preparing them for the more personal profiles that were to follow.

When managers were given their individual feedback reports, they were asked to analyze their own behavior in the same light: given the feedback in fourteen critical competencies, how were their behaviors helping Landmark get to where it wanted to go, and how did they need to change or improve? "We stressed that they didn't have to share their individual feedback," says Burns. "We presented it as simply a way to verify what people were thinking, so it wasn't threatening to the participants." At this stage, each participant identified an individual development goal to work on.

The rest of the program was devoted to the question of how best to manage the change process and what was required to serve as an effective role model for others in the company. First, a process for effective change management was laid out. Then, the participating managers learned about how the behaviors on which they had just received feedback—consulting, inspiring, teambuilding, or networking, for example—could be used to support the change process. In this way, the discussion of how their behavior affected Landmark's culture and how Landmark's goals could be achieved was taken to another level of specificity; they addressed the question, What are the specific behaviors I need to engage in to get us to where we want to go?

As a follow-up to the program, Burns has planned a three-part effort. First, a one-day meeting of all program attendees will be held, at which time they and the meeting's facilitators will review their progress toward achieving their development goals and identify areas for additional coaching. Second, a version of the 360° feedback process will be rolled out among the next level of managers to ensure that everyone gets the same message and is focused on the same critical behaviors. Third, the behaviors identified as characterizing a culture that can support Landmark's strategic direction will be made part of the performance appraisal process. In this way, everyone will be clear about what behaviors are to be evaluated and rewarded.

Fostering Individual Development: Lehrer McGovern Bovis

In 1979, Peter Lehrer and a coworker resigned from a large construction management firm and founded the construction management firm of Lehrer/McGovern in New York. Today, the firm of Bovis, Inc., a U.S. holding company for the London-based Bovis

Construction Group (a subsidiary of Peninsular and Oriental Steam Navigation Company [P&O]), is one of the largest construction management firms in the world. Among the projects it has managed are such high-visibility renovations and restorations as the Statue of Liberty, Ellis Island, and Grand Central Terminal.

Lehrer was inspired to start the firm when he realized that construction management firms often failed to fulfill their commitments to owners. "The idea was that when we made a commitment, we would make sure it was lived up to," Lehrer says, adding, "That's not a technology issue but an attitudinal issue. It means leaving nothing undone to meet the objective."[7]

One key to LMB's success is its emphasis on preconstruction services, which, according to Lehrer, "are something a lot of companies promise but really don't deliver." Instead of passively waiting for information to come its way, LMB attempts to anticipate and act on information as it evolves. "We've spent a lot of money and assigned a lot of people to make it a real service and not a sales technique with nothing behind it,"[8] Lehrer says. This philosophy has become a fundamental element of the company culture, and because of it, LMB is one of the few construction management companies that emphasize providing project managers with formal leadership and interpersonal skills training.

Going beyond LMB's standard curriculum, a special program that used a 360° feedback questionnaire was designed to give the firm's high-potential managers a development opportunity that could foster both their personal and professional growth. As an added benefit, the firm hoped that the feedback received by these people, which focused particularly on leadership skills, would help to prepare them for more senior positions in the organization. The feedback process was therefore seen as both an individual development opportunity and, less directly, a way for the company to ensure that it would have the right people in place to lead the company in the future.

The feedback program was especially important, according to Rich Lupi, Bovis's vice president of human resources, because "the

performance appraisal system in place at that point wasn't comprehensive. The 360° feedback process was seen as a great opportunity
for managers to make sure their people got thorough information
about their performance. And from the point of view of the participants themselves, it was a chance the organization had never given
them before to find out how others really perceived them."[9]

Because the initial offering of the program was specifically targeted at high-potential people, the general reaction within the organization was positive. Managers were pleased to have the chance
to offer their best people "something special." Those who were chosen regarded their selection as a sign of the organization's high opinion of them, as well as a chance to strengthen their skills.

Lupi was in charge of choosing the 360° questionnaire that
Bovis would use as the centerpiece of the program. Since he did not
have the resources to develop his own questionnaire in-house, he
thoroughly examined many of those on the market before choosing
one for use within Bovis. "To me, the most important criterion in
choosing a questionnaire was that it be user friendly, that is, easy for
both the raters and the recipients of the feedback to understand."[10]

The first round of the program was such a success that the
company decided to put all their managers—not just the high-
potentials—through the 360° feedback process. According to Lupi,
the effects of the program were not confined to management practices alone. He actually saw an impact on turnover. "In our organization as a whole, the turnover rate for project managers is about
12 percent. For participants in the 360° program, it was only about 2
percent. That's a pretty remarkable statistic." Lupi also observes, "I
think it has a lot to do with the perception that the organization really values them and is willing to invest in their development. Which
isn't to say there aren't some long faces when the feedback is first presented to them—there always are. But overall, it's one of the best
boosters of self-esteem I know of, because it not only gives them the
opportunity to grow and learn, it also signals to them that the organization is committed to their development. In fact, I think it even
has a positive effect on those who are asked to evaluate others; they
see that their opinions are valued."[11]

Margaret Van Voast, whose experience at the program we described in the preceding chapter, expresses similar enthusiasm. "Last year, I was asked to relocate to another office, and I don't know if I would have felt so ready to take on the challenge if it hadn't been for the confidence I'd gained through going through the program."[12]

Lupi and others within Bovis cite the importance of the group workshops in which the feedback is received and management skills are practiced. In addition to the 360° feedback questionnaire, the training program included a behavioral business simulation that allowed people to practice the critical leadership and management behaviors in a realistic work environment and get additional feedback on the spot. "The simulation used in the workshop helped break down the defenses of any nonbelievers there may have been. They might say to themselves, 'That feedback I got just isn't true; someone had it in for me,' but when they act out their management roles in the simulated company, and the other participants give them the exact same feedback, they can't go on pretending there's no truth in what they've been told about themselves."[13]

At Bovis, the follow-up to the feedback is somewhat informal, but it still takes place. For example, an individual's boss may refer to the development plan that came out of the skills workshop and point out that a certain skill is still not being used or refer back to it to check on progress during the performance appraisal process. The human resource people, too, in their meetings with individuals, frame the discussion of performance in terms of the feedback that was received and the individual's development plan.

Enhancing Team Effectiveness: CIBC Wood Gundy

The Canadian Imperial Bank of Commerce is the second largest bank in Canada and among the ten largest banks in North America. In 1995, it had total assets of $179,244 million; net income was $1,015 million, up 14 percent from the previous year; and return on equity was 12.9 percent, up from 11.7 percent. CIBC is organized into two primary business units—the Personal and Commercial Bank and CIBC Wood Gundy. The Personal and Commercial Bank seeks convenient ways to provide transactional banking to all customers and to deliver specialized financial advisory services to customers with more complex needs. CIBC Wood Gundy provides corporate and investment banking products and services on a global basis.

The formal integration of corporate banking and investment banking operations that formed CIBC Wood Gundy was completed in 1995. The new business structure has enabled the firm to focus better on the customer because of the horizontal integration of the transaction management skills and other skills required to provide client services. Cross-functional client service teams have also been formed to work on providing clients with a complete range of services.

The need for improved cross-organizational teamwork and communication to serve client needs better had been identified several years earlier. Allyn Keiser, then executive vice president of the North American Corporate Bank of CIBC, and his management team wanted to enhance the way account managers, product managers, risk management people, and operations staff worked together to meet their clients' needs.[14] One of the driving forces for this initiative was a customer survey designed to gauge how successfully CIBC was currently serving its clients' changing needs in a highly competitive marketplace. The results of this survey made it clear that the bank was not focusing on its clients in the most organized, efficient way. Instead of coordinating their efforts and their approaches to the customer, product managers and account managers were frequently acting in isolation, which sometimes resulted in redundant efforts or missed opportunities.

There was a feeling among product managers that certain account managers did not bring in the product people until a specific need had already been identified, by which time it was often too late. Account managers, in turn, were leery about bringing product managers to their initial meetings with clients, since they perceived the product managers as too often having a narrow transaction orientation rather than being concerned with the overall client relationship.

At first, it was believed that merely by monitoring the frequency with which account managers brought product managers along on calls and urging the two groups to collaborate more, the situation could be resolved. It soon became apparent, however, that the two groups of managers—as well as the risk management people and the back office people who provided investment and corporate banking services—needed to improve some of the skills required to engage in this kind of collaboration. Specifically, they needed to gain commitment from people over whom they had no direct authority and to work effectively in teams.

Joseph Schmidt, the manager of training and development, was asked to come up with a plan to address this situation. Convinced that skill training would be an important part of the solution, he worked with an outside consulting firm to develop a customized program that would provide people with a model for gaining commitment across functional lines, with feedback on how others currently saw them using the skills necessary for effectively applying the model, and with practice at using the skills they identified as needing further development. A 360° feedback questionnaire was selected to collect people's perceptions of how frequently the skills for teamwork and influencing were currently being used by others.

After the feedback had been collected, the various cross-functional groups had an opportunity to work together in two-day work sessions created especially for that purpose. First, they were presented with the customer survey data to make them more aware of customer needs. Then, they were given the feedback on their effectiveness at teamwork and at gaining commitment from others. This feedback came from their colleagues all around the organization as well as from their bosses. As Keiser puts it, "Before that, we were asking them to change, but we really weren't giving them the tools to take specific corrective action. The 360° feedback was essential for their development."[15]

At the end of the work session, participants focused on using the skills required. In addition to watching videotapes showing the effective use of influencing and teamwork behaviors, they were also given the opportunity to practice their skills using case study exercises that replicated real conditions inside the bank. The exercises reflected the fact that they would not be working in permanent teams when dealing with actual clients but that the teams formed for meeting a particular client's needs might be different each time. Account managers, product managers, risk management people, and back office people all worked together to find creative solutions to the problems presented by the case studies. Team members then gave each other feedback about their use of influencing skills, which reinforced the learning from the feedback provided by their colleagues.

After the workshops, the bank monitored the number of proposals being presented and the extent to which product managers and account managers were going on joint calls and collaborating on meeting customer needs. They found that matters had improved significantly.

As Schmidt later reported, "The feedback definitely made people more aware of what they were doing and how that enhanced or inhibited team effectiveness. It really helped make a difference in the way they worked with each other."[16] Says Keiser, "The feedback helped to ensure that people were focusing on the expectations associated with customer service. In that way, it allowed us to align critical skills with our strategic needs."[17]

Identifying Training and Selection Requirements: Northwestern Mutual Life Insurance Company (NML)

Strong, long-term, steady performance is the hallmark of Northwestern Mutual Life. Throughout its 140-year history, the company has consistently increased its dividend payout to policy holders, while steadily keeping its surplus position well above the norm for the life insurance industry. Its premium income growth and policy holder retention rate have also been excellent, and it has never received anything but the highest rating from A.M. Best Co., Moody's, or Standard & Poor's. NML has achieved these results by steadfastly adhering to the operating principles and business philosophy expressed in an Executive Committee statement of 1888: "The ambition of The Northwestern has been less to be large than to be safe; its aim is to rank first in benefits to policyholders rather than first in size. Valuing quality above quantity, it has preferred to secure its business under certain salutary restrictions and limitations rather than to write much larger business at the possible sacrifice of those valuable points which have made The Northwestern pre-eminently the policyholder's company."

Like most insurance companies nowadays, NML has found itself faced with dramatic industry changes, not least of which is increasing competition for consumers' retirement and savings dollars. As intensified competition and changing demographics put more pressure on the company's financial performance, it has become clear that the historical route to growth—individual agent productivity improvements and opening new general agency offices—is not sufficient. Instead, the general agents contracted by Northwestern Mutual to manage its offices and agents are increasingly being asked to develop their territories by opening additional district agencies.

This change, along with the increased need for market responsiveness and flexibility, is requiring Northwestern's general agents to operate more as leaders than solely as entrepreneurs, as they traditionally were. They now act as strategic leaders of their own agencies and foster, develop, and inspire those who are under contract with them. Since it is not uncommon for general agents to have as many as a hundred agents associated with them, this is a highly demanding task.

Unlike many other insurance companies, however, NML remains fully committed to its use of the general agency as its distribution system. It has therefore had to find a way to ensure that these general agents are equipped for the challenges that confront them and—for selection purposes—to identify the kind of person most likely to succeed as a general agent.

To answer these questions, the company conducted a study to determine the critical success factors for general agents—what leadership and management behaviors had the strongest correlation to exceptional agency performance. David Georgenson, director of field training and development, worked with an outside consulting firm to determine which competencies general agents needed in order to succeed.

The competency model created is being used in two ways, for both development and selection purposes. On the development side, the competency model is being used as the basis for a 360° feedback questionnaire. General agents distribute the questionnaire to the members of their agency teams who serve as their management group, the agents, and members of the home office team that support the general agents in the field. Once the feedback is collected, individual reports are prepared by an outside party. These reports are presented to each general agent in group workshops where they analyze the results and identify their strengths and development needs; the agents then have a chance to practice the crucial behaviors.

For general agents who need extra assistance, one-on-one coaching will be made available by members of the home office's support team. Periodically, these coaches will check back with the general agents to discuss their progress and see if they need any further help. One side benefit of the 360° feedback process has been to reinforce the collaborative, supportive partnership between home office personnel and the general agents.

Meanwhile, the composite feedback report—a consolidation of all the individual data—was used to identify training and development needs for the general agent population as a whole and formed the basis for the curriculum the company has put together to address these general agents' most prevalent training needs.

In addition, the competency model has been formally integrated into the company's selection and appointment process in order to identify those candidates for the general agent position who possess the skills and aptitudes required for success. Rather than continuing to contract with people whose skills might have equipped them only for the more entrepreneurial role the general agents were expected to play in the past, Northwestern is selecting candidates whose leadership and management skills will enable them to be effective in the current environment and can help ensure the company's future success.

Lessons Learned

We asked these practitioners and others what their experiences had taught them about how to make sure that a 360° feedback process achieves its intended objectives. Surprisingly, there was unanimous agreement about five guidelines that should be followed:

Link the effort to a strategic initiative or a business need.

For 360° feedback to be effective as a stimulus for change, people need to understand its broader purpose; only then will you get their initial support and, ultimately, their commitment to the process. "It's never easy to bring about change within an organization," Gail Howard of UJB Financial says, "and we were very aware of the impact our effort could have on some people. At the same time, we saw the program as a genuine source of empowerment for those who stuck with it. It would have been much harder to get people to give the process a fair chance if the relationship to the bank's strategy and the impact on our ability to achieve the business's operating plan were not made clear from the start."[18]

Joe Schmidt, of CIBC Wood Gundy, agrees. "By linking the need for our program to customer survey data, we clearly demonstrated the need for improved teamwork and communication across functional lines. We were then able to show how this improvement would help achieve our business objectives. This got the attention of the managing directors and helped ensure that the program had wide support and great attendance."[19]

Mary Clare Healy, an HRD consultant for management and professional training at Household International, has facilitated a number of 360° feedback programs at Household and noticed a marked change in participants' attitudes when the use of a feedback questionnaire was specifically linked to culture change. "Once we customized our questionnaire specifically to the nineteen success factors that support the values and performance expectations at Household, it had much more meaning for people, and the level of enthusiasm rose dramatically. We have encountered much less resistance in our development-oriented workshops since we built the feedback around the success factors. In addition, knowing that the senior team participated in identifying the success factors and defining what it means to be a leader at Household has made it much easier to get people to focus on the messages contained in the feedback."[20]

Get senior management to participate in and drive the effort.

Everyone we spoke to agreed that the support of senior management was crucial to the success of the process. Management support sends the clearest message to the rest of the organization about the importance of the effort and the role it will play in individual and organizational development. "When the managing directors expressed an interest in attending the program with their teams and receiving the 360° feedback themselves," says Schmidt of CIBC Wood Gundy, "it immediately became an important business initiative and not just something coming out of the HR department."[21]

Managers who are about to receive 360° feedback frequently ask, "Did they do this yet?" referring to more senior people in the organization. If the feedback is seen as something the top tells the middle to do to the bottom, it is less likely to have the intended effect. The rallying cry of resistance becomes, "If it's not required for them, why do I have to do it? They need it as much as anyone." Ed Wiseman, director of Training and Development at The Geon Company, was very aware of this potential problem. "We had senior people participate in the process," he says. "The idea of 360° feedback was then associated with senior executives, so there was less resistance among others in the company. Their participation gave it credibility."[22]

As Mary Clare Healy observes, "On the first round of the change initiative, we began with middle managers. During the current phase, with the "Leaders at all Levels" program, we began with senior managers, and it has made an enormous difference. Before people go through the program, they have to meet with their bosses to talk about their expectations. Now, senior managers who went through the process themselves are meeting with their direct reports who are about to take the program, and they're really taking it seriously and generating a lot of excitement."[23]

Involvement by senior management also helps to ensure that sufficient resources will be made available to support the effort and that the organization will remain committed to the intervention until it achieves its objective. "We are very lucky to have a president who is such a proponent of training and development," says Rich Lupi of Lehrer McGovern Bovis. "Jim D'Agostino consistently ensures that resources are allocated to developing people in the organization. I think it's because he's a learner himself, and he had some very positive experiences with 360° feedback early in his career."[24]

Senior management's participation in the feedback process also helps ensure that the behaviors and competencies that are being measured will be reinforced day-to-day. As Dave Burns of the Landmark Stock Exchange reports, "In our organization we knew that the best way to gain forward momentum and to ensure that the lessons of the program would stick was to start with the most senior group. It was a bit of a risk, because they could have decided this stuff wasn't for them. But we provided them with any information they required about the process and addressed all their initial concerns, including confidentiality and whether people would take the feedback seriously and use it to change behavior. In the end, they were the most enthusiastic participants. As a result, they are clearly reinforcing the relevant behaviors in their daily interactions with their peers and direct reports."

Emphasize clear and frequent communication about the initiative's purpose and implications for each member of the organization.

When it comes to gaining support for the use of 360° feedback, all the people we spoke with agreed with the old maxim, You can't communicate too much or too often. "There were a number of times," says Gary Zambardino, manager of training and development at Bayer Pharmaceuticals, "when we had to go in and explain to the organization how our team development effort was relevant to people's day-to-day work. Even so, when we were given the OK to go ahead, we still had to sell the idea to the groups who were to be the initial participants in the process."[25]

The more people understand about why 360° feedback is being introduced in the organization and how the information will be used, the more likely they are to support the effort, or at least not actively resist it. "One thing I would have done differently," says Gail Howard, of UJB Financial, "is communicate more broadly a little sooner with the various departments from which we needed support. Ultimately, we did have terrific support, and everyone pulled together. But maybe I should have spent more time meeting with them and making sure they understood earlier."[26]

Ensure that people see the behaviors that will be measured as important and relevant to their jobs.

It is much easier to gain people's commitment to the use of 360° feedback if they believe the behaviors that will be measured are directly related to the effective performance of their jobs. "When we decided to go forward with this project, we knew we had to involve the general agents," says David Georgenson of Northwestern Mutual Life. "Not only do they have the greatest insight into what it takes to do the job well, they had to believe that what we were measuring was what was most important to their success at their work."[27]

Although most people will still feel some reluctance toward receiving feedback on their performance, a clear link between the behaviors being measured and their effectiveness on the job helps people get over that hurdle. Margaret Van Voast, the project manager at Lehrer McGovern Bovis, supports this idea when she says, "Even though I was anxious at the beginning, in retrospect it was one of the best things that the company did for me. It gave me a chance to grow and learn and be a better manager, which is what they are paying me to do. It's one of those things where you get out of it what you put into it. I think it was really invaluable to me as a manager."[28]

Provide ongoing support and follow-up.

All the practitioners to whom we spoke felt that the most essential factor for long-term success was building in a follow-up activity or process at the outset of the project. People need clarity about what is expected of them after they receive the feedback, as well as ongoing support, if what they have learned is going to lead to action or change.

It is generally agreed that people need specific development plans for leveraging the strengths and addressing the weaknesses identified by the feedback: they must understand exactly what they are expected to do, and with whom. As Gary Zambardino of Bayer Pharmaceuticals learned, "When we first implemented our 360° feedback process, we didn't ask people to come back with a plan, so it just became air, and we had no way of knowing what was going on after they left. Now we ask them to come back in twenty-one days with a plan. This way we can follow up, and they see us as a value-added resource to help them achieve their targets."[29]

The degree of follow-up and the form it takes depend on both the internal resources available and the motivation of the individual. As Lupi reports, "We weren't able to do as much follow-up as we would have liked because of the size of the HR staff. In an ideal world, their bosses would have done it, but that's contingent on how much information they shared with the boss when they returned from the program. Once they've completed a development plan, there is no formal follow-up. People who are self-motivated will take the opportunity to develop themselves. People who aren't going to pay attention to it—well, their careers may reflect that and be affected by that."[30]

Most people we spoke with feel that a formal follow-up effort produces better results than leaving it up to the individual's discretion whether or not to take a next step. Gail Howard of UJB Financial, which used a more formal follow-up process, observes, "This program would never have succeeded without the coordination of many groups and departments. We needed managers at all levels of the organization to commit to have follow-up meetings, we needed the support of corporate training and development to ensure that skill development opportunities were in place, and we needed each participant to take the next steps on his or her development plan in order to close any gaps."[31]

Concluding Remarks

A key factor that contributed to the success of the 360° feedback processes described above was that these organizations had a clear sense of what they wanted to accomplish through the use of feedback. In each case, there was a well-defined goal that enabled those involved in designing and implementing the process to identify which skills and practices would be emphasized both when gathering the information and when coaching the participants.

In our experience, this focus on goals—the why of the process—is of paramount importance in deciding on the hows and the whos that will make the program maximally effective. Processes that are initiated for uncertain reasons almost inevitably achieve uncertain results.

Chapter Three

The Most Important
Decision You Will Make

Choosing a Method for Collecting the Feedback

> There is a way to do it better—find it.
> —*Thomas A. Edison, to a research associate*

As we explained in Chapter One, questionnaires and interviews are the two most popular methods for collecting feedback from multiple sources, and each can be used either alone or in conjunction with the other. In this chapter and the one following, we will discuss the factors to consider when making your decision about which approach to use and offer some pointers on how to use each method to maximum effect.

Questionnaires

Questionnaires gather feedback in the form of numerical or quantitative ratings on specific behaviors or personal characteristics. For each question, the rater is given a choice of responses, which usually take the form of a range of options that ask raters how frequently (for example, always to never) or how well (for example, very well to very poorly) the behavior is used or to what extent (for example, a great extent to not at all) the manager in question displays a certain characteristic. Raters select the response that best fits their perceptions, based on their experiences with the manager and their observations of his or her behavior.

Many questionnaires contain a standard set of items geared toward general populations such as senior managers, supervisors, project leaders, or individual contributors. However, instruments targeted at specific individuals or functions in an organization are being developed all the time. Ten years ago, there were only twenty or thirty questionnaires on the market; today there are over one hundred. The existence of so many different instruments is another indication of how many different uses organizations have found for multi-rater feedback.[1]

Some questionnaires also include open-ended questions that call for written comments from the respondents. Questions such as, "What does this person do that is most effective in this area of behavior?" or "What could this person do that would be more effective?" enable respondents to elaborate on the quantitative answers they have given. Because additional questions mean it will take longer to complete the questionnaire, we often recommend having a single open-ended item at the end of the questionnaire. Including just one item such as, "What can this person do to be more effective when working with you?" can add enormously to the value of the feedback.

As noted in Chapter Two, Dave Burns, the managing director of human resource planning and development at the Landmark Stock Exchange, felt the inclusion of an open-ended question at the end of the feedback questionnaire made all the difference. "The information they got from the open-ended item," he says, "was the most powerful part of the day. It had very high impact." The senior managers at Landmark seemed to agree. One of them remarked, "The numerical data are interesting and helpful, but when you read how people see you as a leader and what they'd like to see you do more and less of, in their own words, it's mind blowing. It's really great stuff."[2]

Interviews

Most interviews used for 360° feedback are conducted one-on-one, in private settings, and can last anywhere from half an hour to three hours. To obtain the best results, the interviewer should usually be a professional facilitator, consultant, or psychologist trained in both interviewing techniques and the analysis of the information that is generated.

Like the open-ended questions on questionnaires, interviews tend to yield very rich qualitative data. Although the interviewer generally uses a structured format of prepared questions, many of them are indeed open-ended; the interviewer will thus hear broad opinions and perceptions and can then probe for concrete examples and clarify answers that could be interpreted more than one way. At the same time, more specific questions are used to elicit information about particular areas of behavior. Once all the responses are collected, the interviewer analyzes them to extract themes, patterns, and key messages and prepares a report of the findings. The report may also include recommendations for improvement.

While the two methods of data collection differ in their form and the type of information they produce, they are far from being mutually exclusive. Used in combination, they can create a picture of an individual's behavior and its impact on others that neither method could produce on its own.

Choosing the Method That Will Work Best for You

Each method has its strengths and weaknesses. Although both are highly effective, questionnaires tend to be more widely used because they are easier to administer and less costly. They are also easier to score and have greater (or at least better established) reliability and validity. As you think about the method, or combination of methods, that is most appropriate for you, you will need to keep in mind the number of people who will receive feedback, the organizational level with which you are working, the type of data you will be collecting, and the resources you have available—budget, time, personnel, and expertise.

The Number of People Who Will Receive Feedback

Let us say you are working with an individual manager, Andrea Johnson, on her personal and professional development and have decided, with her agreement, that 360° feedback would be a useful way to gain insight into her behavior. Ms. Johnson is the leader of a business team consisting of five direct reports. Along with seven other colleagues, she is a member of her boss's business team; she also works with dozens of colleagues in other functions and business units across the company. These activities give her many possible sources for feedback. At a minimum, you want to gather perceptions of her behavior and effectiveness from about ten people—four direct reports, five colleagues, and her boss (or some similar combination).

For each manager slated to receive feedback, you will have to collect and analyze data from ten people, not including the manager. If you are working with a group of ten managers, you will need to collect data from at least one hundred people. As you can see, the magnitude of the effort can be daunting. So what is the best approach—interviews or questionnaires?

When you are working with large populations, questionnaires are a far more efficient method for collecting data, since they usually come prepackaged and only need to be distributed with instructions for how to complete them and when and where to return them. You can easily involve greater numbers of respondents, although we find that eight to ten people are usually sufficient. The time required to collect the data is significantly less than with the interview method, and the data analysis is faster, because it is based on quantifiable items. Furthermore, most questionnaires use computer scoring programs to aggregate the data and produce the reports.

Level in the Organization

For individuals or small groups of senior executives and high-potential middle managers, you may want to invest the time and money required for the interview method. The flexibility of the interview approach enables you to get at the unique aspects of the senior executive's role and the demands of the job and provides rich anecdotal data that help people better understand how they are seen by others. The presentation of the findings, which usually takes place in a one-on-one meeting, allows for a more in-depth discussion of strengths, weaknesses, and next steps. Such a setting also provides an opportunity to explore the need for change and examine highly focused strategies for change most suited to people in senior positions. For example, it might enable an executive to go beyond simply identifying networking as an area in need of development to discussing why better networking is needed as he manages the launch of a new business venture. And he can see how to network more effectively.

The Type of Data to Be Collected

Some types of data are more easily collected by questionnaire, while others are best collected through interviews. If you are primarily interested in gathering information on people's skills and knowledge—their current abilities—a questionnaire may be the most efficient way to go. The multiple-choice construction of a questionnaire works very well when collecting people's perceptions of how frequently or how well specific, observable behaviors are being used. While this type of information can also be collected through interviews, and the data may be richer because of the interviewer's ability to probe for more detail, additional information may not be worth the time and resources you will have to devote to get it.

If the focus of your data collection is on recipients' potential or their style or personality characteristics, multiple-choice questionnaires may not provide enough information. To get an accurate picture of their ability to learn and to apply what they have learned or to see how their patterns of behavior play out, interviews may be necessary and worth the time and resources they require. Unlike questionnaires, interviews allow you to ask follow-up questions to get at the nuances of a person's style and its impact on others. It is harder to anticipate the second- or third-level questions you would need to ask to get this type of information when developing a questionnaire.

The Resources You Have Available

In deciding which approach to use, you will first need to consider the total time available to complete the project and the amount of time you can allocate per feedback recipient. Obviously, the more recipients you have, the more time you will require to collect, process, and present the findings. Most questionnaires can be distributed, returned, and processed (with reports prepared) within six weeks. Presenting the data will take about five working days for every one hundred people (five one-day sessions for twenty people each). If you are using interviews, you will require about six working days per recipient (one day to schedule the interviews, two days to conduct the interviews, one day to analyze the data, one day to prepare the report, and one day to review the findings and prepare a development plan).

The number of people you can dedicate to the project and the degree of expertise they possess will be another important consideration. As we have indicated, the interview method, although highly effective, is labor-intensive. It also requires a certain level of expertise to conduct an effective interview and make sense of the data that have been collected. Furthermore, for the interviewing and presentation process to be truly effective, the interviewer must have the complete trust of the recipient and the people from whom the data will be collected. It can be expensive to use outside resources for this type of work, either to obtain expertise, to augment internal staff, or to assure recipients and respondents that the data will be treated confidentially.

The questions of time and resources take us to the important consideration of budget. As mentioned earlier, questionnaires tend to be less expensive—the same budget dollars do not go as far using the interview method. With larger groups, volume discounts based on the number of questionnaires can drive the per-person cost even lower.

Apart from budget issues, resource availability is the primary reason people select the questionnaire method—it does not require a lot of skilled personnel to administer or prepare reports of the findings.

Selecting a Questionnaire

Choosing a data collection method, or a combination of methods, is only the beginning of the decision-making process. If you have determined that a questionnaire is the right way to go for your needs, you must now identify the best questionnaire for the job. This is no small task. With so many options available, making an informed choice is more important but more difficult than ever.

So, how do you go about finding the right instrument, one that will provide the feedback to address your specific set of organizational needs? Just as organizations have a particular focus and area of expertise, so do questionnaires. Look, therefore, for a high degree of correlation between the questionnaire you choose and the management philosophy of your organization, as well as the goals you want to achieve.

The search for a suitable instrument will generally consist of two stages—the initial search, which will eliminate all but a few of the available questionnaires, and the in-depth evaluation of those that remain.[3]

The Initial Search

The purpose of the initial search is to narrow the field of possibilities. The following guidelines will help with this process:

1. Clarify the purpose of the intervention and what you want people to get out of the feedback. What do you want people to understand or do differently?

2. Obtain samples of the materials—the instrument itself, the feedback report, the support materials, and so forth.

3. Determine whether the model or theory on which the questionnaire is based—represented by the scales on which people receive feedback—matches your needs and is consistent with your organization's norms and values. (A task force made up of representatives from the different units in which the instrument will be used may be best suited to make this determination, and involving potential participants will also help to build acceptance.)

4. Review the instrument and the feedback report for clarity and face validity.

5. Find out the cost both in time and dollars for administering the questionnaire, processing the data, and preparing the reports.

6. Eliminate instruments based on a theoretical model that is inconsistent with the needs and values of your organization or whose cost exceeds your available budget.

Clarify What People Need to Do Differently. Let us assume, for example, that there is general agreement that people in your organization need to improve their leadership and management skills. By identifying the leadership and managerial practices that contribute most directly to the success of your organization, you can save yourself time when shopping around for a suitable instrument. Because it is good policy to have a list of specific areas in mind when looking at feedback instruments, you can draw up your own list of what you consider to be key practices, based on your knowledge and experience; in addition, you may wish to consult outside studies of what makes for a successful manager. Identifying key leadership and managerial practices will help you determine which questionnaire is most closely pegged to the management philosophy of your organization. (You may want to confirm your list with key managers from the different business units.)

Providing feedback on behaviors that are not significant factors in what you want to achieve is a waste of time and money. Therefore, once you have decided which managerial behaviors are of the greatest importance to your organization, see which of the questionnaires elicit the most feedback around these practices. The key is finding an instrument whose categories match up with your organization's goals.

Remember: the feedback questionnaire is more than just a means to an end; it is an intrinsic part of the feedback process whose form and content help shape the feedback and what may result from it. When chosen wisely, it can be a highly effective instrument for bringing about meaningful organizational change.

Obtain Samples of the Materials. There are several useful guides containing information on the questionnaires that are available—information about what they measure and how to obtain sample materials.[4]

The American Psychological Association guidelines require that certain information be readily available when an instrument is offered for sale. When you are collecting information on a product, be sure you request a sample of the questionnaire that will be used for self-evaluation and the version that is used for each respondent group, if different; a sample of the feedback report that people will use to review and interpret the data; support materials, including a participant's manual, job aids, and a trainer's guide; the technical report that describes how the questionnaire was developed; and information on the price of the questionnaire and the fees charged for processing the data and conducting the workshops in which it will be presented to participants.

This is your first screening criterion: any firm that cannot supply these materials should be eliminated from consideration.

You should also ask for names and telephone numbers of several recent clients and ask those clients about their experiences with the instrument and the firm. Do not hesitate to ask pointed questions.

Is the Theoretical Model Consistent with Your Needs? Every questionnaire available on the market will be based on a theory or model of leadership and management effectiveness, team effectiveness, or interpersonal effectiveness. The description of this theory or model will usually be somewhere in the technical report or in the materials where an overview of the model is provided to the recipients of the feedback. You will need to review the model to understand what it includes. Does it provide people with feedback on their behavior? On their leadership style? On their knowledge and skills such as financial ability or strategic thinking? Does it focus on personal characteristics like energy level or emotional stability? Is the model appropriate for the level of people who will be using it? Does it emphasize the competencies that are important to your organization?

Refer to the technical report to learn how the scales were drawn up. How were the items chosen to form a scale or category? Scale development is based on theoretical, statistical, and rational-intuitive methods. The theoretical is predicated upon a proposed model of effective leadership and management; the statistical is derived from research data; the rational-intuitive makes use of the authors' workplace experience and expectations.

In our experience, using all three methods creates scales that produce the best results, that is, items that have a sound theoretical and statistical underpinning and reflect what real people do in the real world. It is critical to determine the genesis of scales, because you will be asking managers to use the information generated by these scales to change their behaviors. Therefore, make sure that the skills, behaviors, and attributes measured by the instrument actually relate to job effectiveness in your organization.

Now, check to see how the instrument allocates its items to compare your intended use to the instrument's characteristics. What is the instrument's *target audience* and what is its *norm group* (its basis for comparison)? If such a norm group exists, what kind and level of people supplied the initial data that are stored in the vendor's database? The pitfalls are obvious. If the group you want to measure is composed primarily of middle managers, and the norm group was made up of senior managers (for whom the items are more applicable), the ensuing scores will in all probability be lower than scores derived from an instrument whose norm group was other middle managers. An instrument targeting all managerial levels might not be right for middle managers in your organization, if only because the competencies assessed are not in line with your management goals for this group.

This is your second screening criterion: any questionnaires that do not meet the profile of your target population and deal with the competencies that are important to your organization should be eliminated from consideration.

Confirm Face Validity. For any questionnaire under consideration, you will want to be sure of two things—that the questions are clear and unambiguous and that the target population perceives them to be relevant to their jobs. In our experience, the best way to confirm face validity is to show the sample questionnaire to a representative group of the people who will be giving and receiving the feedback (you may even ask them to complete the questionnaire on their bosses to better form an opinion). These people are in the best position to help determine the extent to which the items are seen as important and easy to understand and observe.

There is some risk involved in this approach. The sample population may reject all the possible choices, because they feel the behaviors do not represent their unique situation, or they are uncomfortable with the idea of receiving feedback on any aspect of their performance. We believe, however, that involving the target population early in the decision-making process is worth the risk. When people have a say in selecting the questionnaire that will be used to measure their performance, it contributes to gaining their commitment and buy-in and increases the likelihood that they will be open to the information that the questionnaire provides.

This is your third screening criterion: if members of the target group do not feel the questionnaire works for them, you may as well move on to other options. Even if you believe they are wrong, you will be setting yourself up for a series of battles along the way and, possibly, the rejection of the feedback once you get to that point in the process.

Price Considerations. Selecting an instrument that fits your budget is an important consideration, but quality should be considered in relation to price. A careful comparison of instruments and their support materials can often clarify the real cost of the product, what you are getting for your money, and how that compares to other products. Some questionnaires of equal quality may not be competitively priced. Some may offer features and options that you do not value, making their per-head cost too high relative to other questionnaires. Some products may have hidden costs—features that are standard on one product but call for an additional fee on another. Examples are composite reports or additional questionnaires for respondents and time spent answering questions or resolving problems. Many suppliers offer volume discounts that can minimize the per-person cost. Taking another tack, you may decide to limit the number of people you initially involve in order to stay within cost parameters.

This is your fourth screening criterion: questionnaires that are of the same quality as less expensive options, and meet your needs no better, should be eliminated.

The In-depth Evaluation

An in-depth evaluation of each of the instruments that remain will enable you to determine which features are most important to you and which questionnaire has the combination of features that will best meet your needs. In addition to the questionnaire, you will also need to evaluate the feedback report and the support materials. Ask yourself the following:

Is the Questionnaire Well Researched?   A theoretical model is no more than a hypothesis until it has been tested. There are many models of leadership and management described in countless books on the subject—many of them, unfortunately, not very good. And of the many instruments now based on these models, probably no more than one in four has been professionally developed and adequately tested for validity and reliability. Empirical research should show how each behavior itemized on the questionnaire is related to effectiveness.

How important is it, really, for an instrument to be adequately tested for these characteristics? It may seem that face validity is enough. After all, these questionnaires have been developed every year by smart people who ought to know what effective leaders and managers do. But when you ask people to use the feedback they receive to change their behavior, you are implicitly asking them to trust that the instrument is relevant and well constructed. Solid evidence that the behaviors being assessed are relevant for success increases people's interest in getting and using the feedback. In fact, some managers in your organization may refuse to give credence to your effort until they confirm for themselves that there is a sound scientific basis for the assessment. Your supplier should be willing to provide technical materials and to answer questions about the research methods used.

Our view is that the soundness of the instrument is one of the most important considerations when selecting a questionnaire. We also recognize that poring over technical reports is a time-consuming and daunting task for many people. There are, however, two relatively simple things to look for to determine the questionnaire's soundness—reliability and validity.

An instrument's reliability can be judged by assessing its consistency in three key areas—test-retest consistency, internal consistency, and inter-rater agreement.[5] Let us look at each briefly.

Test-retest consistency is a measure of the instrument's stability over time. Would raters' scores be the same over a short period if there were no change in behavior on the part of the person being rated? If Jane answers an item about Bob in one way today, would she select the same response tomorrow? Because of their wording, some items have higher stability over time than others. For example, an item like "tends to be conservative" might have a low test-retest reliability. If Jane has just seen Bob allocate a huge sum of money for a risky project, she might say he is not conservative. But a week later, if the two of them have a conversation about politics, she might characterize Bob as conservative, although Bob's behavior on the job has in no way changed.

Some questionnaire authors claim that test-retest studies are irrelevant, since their instruments are designed to promote change.

They contend that if Jane's opinion of Bob is different the second time around, it only shows how effective the initial feedback was at getting him to change his behavior. This argument ducks the issue of measurement. You cannot use an instrument to measure change unless you know that the items or scales will remain constant under conditions of *no* change. To find out about an instrument's stability over time, look in the technical report under the section titled, "Test-Retest Reliability." The numbers for each scale and item should be a minimum of .5, and .6 is generally considered good for a feedback instrument.[6]

The second criterion of reliability relates to the scales on which the feedback will be given. Internal consistency means that all the items in a given scale truly measure the same competency and that there are sufficient items to measure it adequately. If all the items measure the same skill, it is only logical that people who exhibit one of the behaviors that define the scale will also exhibit the other behaviors. Internal consistency should be in the .65 to .85 range. If the reliability coefficient is low, either the scale contains too few items or the items have too little in common. If it is very high, the scale may contain more items than necessary.[7]

The third type of consistency is inter-rater agreement—how much agreement is there among people (for example, colleagues) who are likely to see the person similarly? While raters with different perspectives (peers versus direct reports) may disagree on their assessment of the person, raters with the same perspective should show at least moderate agreement. Very low inter-rater agreement may indicate that the scale lacks clarity. Do not, however, expect inter-rater reliability to be as high in statistical terms as other measures of reliability. Regardless of how well constructed a questionnaire is, most raters are untrained observers and will understand and interpret items differently. Statistically, .5 is considered a high degree of inter-rater agreement.[8]

Whereas the test of reliability is consistency, the test of validity is integrity. The integrity of a questionnaire lies in its accuracy at measuring what it is designed to measure, as well as the relevance of what it measures to real-life job performance. Indeed, if we do not know that the instrument we are using is valid, why should we expect people to take it seriously enough to use it as a basis for change? The most convincing evidence of validity will be that scores on the instrument are related to data from an independent source: actual performance appraisals, perhaps, or objective measures of work unit performance. These kinds of data are not always available, so many instruments use ratings from the same source. That is, the same people who rated the person on the instrument being tested are asked to rate him or her on some different scale of overall effectiveness or performance as well.

In the technical report, headings may refer to different kinds of validity (construct, content, concurrent, and so on) but look for evidence of at least one study showing a significant relationship between scores on the instrument and some measure of actual effectiveness on the job. The details of the study and its results should be fully described.

How Are the Questions Structured? When selecting a questionnaire, look for the following qualities:[9]

Behavioral: The items on the questionnaire should describe specific, observable behaviors. People have difficulty giving accurate feedback when behaviors are described in vague, general terms such as, "Structures the work roles of direct reports." The items should describe concrete behaviors. Examples are "Explains what results are expected when a task is assigned," or "Tells you when a task you are doing needs to be completed." Specific items like these provide the basis for feedback that is easy for people to interpret and use.

Positive: Behaviors should be described in positive rather than negative terms. Avoid questionnaires with items like, "Yells at you for making a mistake." Better wording would be, "Helps you understand the reason for a mistake." Some direct reports will be leery of reporting that their boss does something that is ineffective (even if he does so only occasionally); they are more likely to say he does not use an effective behavior frequently. Moreover, a questionnaire with lots of negative items tends to make people feel defensive and less likely to participate in the feedback process. Finally, feedback about ineffective behavior does not tell people what they should be doing, only what not to do.

Personal: Whenever feasible, behavior should be described in terms related to the individual answering the questionnaire. It is better, for example, to ask for a response to "This manager praises me when I carry out a task effectively" than "This manager praises direct reports who carry out a task effectively." Respondents should not be expected to hazard guesses about a person's behavior with others. This kind of wording also gives a more accurate picture when the person behaves differently toward different people. Of course, such wording is not appropriate for behaviors that involve more than one person ("Holds a special celebration after the group successfully accomplishes a project") or for behaviors the person performs alone ("Reviews performance reports for the work unit").

Multidirectional: Very few people behave exactly the same with their bosses or colleagues as with their direct reports. That is why feedback from different perspectives provides a more complete picture of the person's behavior. But do not solicit 360° feedback on behaviors that are used exclusively in one type of relationship. Delegating, for example, is something managers do with direct reports. Colleagues and bosses will generally not have first-hand knowledge of a manager's delegating behaviors. Thus, you may need different versions of the questionnaire for respondents with different relationships to the manager. On the other hand, an instrument that meets your needs in all other respects need not be excluded from consideration merely because it contains a scale that is relevant to only one group of respondents. The feedback process can be managed to accommodate this.

The Feedback Report

Once you are satisfied of an instrument's reliability and validity, it is time to examine the feedback report. This will give you a sense of how much and what kind of information the person will get, as well as the form in which it is presented.

The presentation of feedback data can take any number of forms and usually involves some trade-offs. Very short instruments, for example, will have very short displays. The obvious trade-off here is that while a short display makes for quicker interpretation, it offers less information. Does it go deep enough? A very long display, on the other hand, may offer too much information, even nonessential data, making interpretation difficult or confusing.

When checking the data display, determine how successfully it safeguards rater confidentiality. (Are there at least three respondents in each rater group? Are the responses to open-ended questions edited to protect the identity of the author?) This can be especially important if raters are aware of how the display is formatted, since awareness that a particular format does not ensure anonymity may make them give less than honest feedback.

We have found that confidentiality usually becomes a thorny issue when feedback from the boss is presented separately. If, for example, there is only one boss, then his or her rating of a person's competencies will be out in the open. To avoid misunderstandings, this fact should be made clear before a multi-rater questionnaire is distributed. As for peers and direct reports, the greater number involved in rating, the greater the feeling of confidentiality, especially if the display reinforces such feelings.

There are many ways to summarize respondents' feedback, some of them more useful than others. In general, however, the feedback report should:[10]

Identify the behaviors that are considered most important to the effective performance of the person's job.

Importance ratings for each of the practices provide focus and direction for further analysis of the data. They also show the extent to which the recipient and other key stakeholders agree on what it takes to be successful in a particular position or situation. Not surprisingly, our experience has shown that people tend to be most interested in their boss's ratings of importance. The comparison of what they think is vital to their effectiveness to their boss's opinion is useful both for understanding their boss's perspective on how their jobs should be done and as the basis for further discussion and development planning.

Clearly identify feedback from different perspectives.

Behavior descriptions obtained from different perspectives—direct reports, colleagues, bosses—should be presented separately. Aggregating feedback from different sources tends to make it more difficult to interpret. For example, if a manager tends to use consultation frequently with colleagues but seldom with direct reports, aggregate data will obscure the fact that the manager treats people differently, according to their relationship to him or her.

Compare feedback from others with the person's own perspective.

Most feedback reports compare what others say about a person's behavior to self-ratings by the person on a parallel questionnaire. Just going through the process of rating themselves helps people understand their behavior better. Comparing their own ratings to those of others also helps people interpret the feedback. A high level of agreement among the various raters confirms that the person's self-assessment need not be re-examined; major disagreement suggests that more probing is necessary to learn the cause of the discrepancies.

People often rate themselves higher than others rate them. For example, a manager may indicate that direct reports are frequently praised for their accomplishments, whereas the direct reports indicate that they receive little recognition from the manager. This is exactly the type of discrepancy that should get the manager's attention and probably indicates a weakness to be addressed. However, it is important to explore the reasons for the discrepancy rather than jumping to conclusions about it. Self-ratings may be higher because a manager is biased, or certain behaviors may not be visible to the other raters, or the other raters may have interpreted the item differently. A discrepancy in the other direction may also occur, although this is less common. For example, managers may rate themselves lower than others do on inspiring direct reports to greater efforts, perhaps because they do not realize the extent of their positive influence as leaders.

Compare the person's ratings to norms.

It is difficult for a manager to know whether a score on a specific behavior is high or low without some way of comparing it to other people's scores. For example, since most people use rational persuasion very frequently when they try to influence others, a below-average score on this behavior will not be obvious without the use of norms. One effective way to show where an individual manager falls in the distribution of scores for a large sample of people is to use a percentile score that indicates how many people in the database got lower scores. It is important to be sure that the population making up the norm group is similar to the people who are receiving the feedback—does the norm group consist of senior managers or middle managers or technical professionals or a general population? Is it made up of people from your industry or a representative sample that cuts across industries?

Display feedback for items as well as scales.

Most behavior scales or categories consist of several items. The behavior scale of Mentoring, for example, may consist of items such as, "Offers helpful advice on how to advance your career," "Provides you with opportunities to develop your skills and demonstrate what you can do," "Encourages you to attend relevant training programs, workshops, or night courses to develop greater skill and expertise," and "Provides extra instruction or coaching to help you improve your job skills and learn new ones."

Some feedback reports provide feedback for the scales but not for the separate items they contain. Both types of feedback are useful. Item feedback helps people better understand the behavior scales and reduces the problems caused by missing responses. Once the scale scores have been computed, the fact that different respondents skipped different items that make up the scale is camouflaged. Managers may then interpret omitted responses as an indication that a behavior is never performed, which can skew the feedback.

The best form of item feedback is a mean score for each item (the ratings from all respondents on the item are totaled and divided by the number of respondents), plus one of several other measures to help the recipient understand the range of responses. Some feedback reports also present a range of scores (highest and lowest) and the distribution of answers from different respondents (how many people in each group selected which response). Again, the score distribution should not be shown unless there are enough respondents to protect their anonymity.

Include recommendations.

Feedback questionnaires typically ask respondents to describe what the manager does, not what the respondent would like the manager to do. We have found that asking respondents for recommendations provides a useful supplement to feedback about observed behavior. Recommendations that show how many respondents said the manager should use the behavior more frequently, the same amount, or less help recipients interpret the feedback and identify their strengths and weaknesses. For example, although someone might have a moderately high score on delegating to direct reports, certain direct reports may prefer even more delegation. Without the recommendation, it would be hard to discover this opportunity for improvement. Occasionally, respondents think a person should use a behavior less, although this does not happen as often if the questionnaire describes only positive behaviors. Because of the extra time required to complete a questionnaire that calls for recommendations, these questions should focus on scales rather than individual items.

Benefits of Interpretive Frameworks

Suppose we are using an instrument with five feedback scales: Planning, Delegating, Getting Information, Influencing, and Self-management, on which a hypothetical manager has ratings (on a 5-point scale) as shown in Exhibit 3.1.[11]

Without balancing or qualifying information, the manager might conclude that 3.8 is a satisfactory score for Influencing, especially since it confirms his self-rating. But what if another scale existed, rating the importance of Influencing, that showed that most raters considered it an extremely important skill for managers to have? Wouldn't this affect the way this manager now regarded his score? Or what if he knew that the norm for all managers was 4.5? Suddenly, a score of 3.8 takes on a whole different meaning.

Now, consider Planning. Awarded a 4.5 rating by others, the manager should be pleased with himself (the rater score is even higher than his self-rating of 4.0). But what if the rater response does not reflect approval so much as the perception that this manager is always initiating plans, even making busy work for himself and others? Another scale addressing what the manager should "do more" or "do less" might reveal that raters think he should do less planning or a more directed type of planning. Maybe his direct reports are feeling smothered by his managerial style.

Exhibit 3.1. Example of Feedback on a 5-Point Scale

Scale	Average of Rater Responses	Self-Rating
Planning	4.5	4.0
Delegating	4.4	5.0
Getting information	4.0	4.2
Influencing	3.8	3.9
Self-management	2.1	3.1

Not atypically, this person overrated himself on four out of five areas. Left to his own devices, he will probably pay attention to self-rater differences greater than .4, as with Self-management. But how can he know whether the gap for Getting Information is large enough to cause concern? Feedback can be enriched when it shows which self-rater differences should be considered significant.

Finally, it is difficult to understand how to change or improve competencies defined in abstract terms. Self-management is an example. Does a score of 2.1 on Self-management mean that raters think this manager is unaware of his own strengths and weaknesses? Or that he is spreading himself too thin? Feedback on the item level rather than just the scale level would be very useful here. In other words, how did raters respond to the specific, concrete behavioral examples on the questionnaire that were combined to form the Self-management scale?

Most instruments do not make use of all these strategies for interpretation, and you need not look for one that does. However, three or more in a single instrument are preferable to give recipients a context in which to interpret responses.

The Support Materials

The final area to consider is the quality of the support materials provided for both feedback recipients and the person who will work with them to help them understand the data and determine appropriate next steps. The key questions to ask about support materials include:

Do the support materials explain how to make the most of the data? Do they help managers ascertain key areas for improvement and plan their next steps?

The final criterion of instrument selection relates to the use to which the data will be put. As you review the support materials, see if they include information on how feedback recipients can make constructive use of it. After all, even good information placed in the hands of people who do not know what to make of it becomes useless information. They should explain both the model and how managers can improve performance based on specific data. This information will come in the form of a participant manual or binder, along with development guides that contain tips and pointers for improvement. You should be satisfied that the material is well written, is easy to understand and use, and reflects the values and goals of your organization.

Is there adequate guidance and support for trainers administering the feedback? Are the scoring method and its implications spelled out?

Another consideration is the quality of support for trainers. A good instrument includes materials that guide a trainer in using and interpreting the data. This material should also explain clearly how the quantitative results are arrived at, how the instrument is scored—by the vendor? by you? by the managers themselves?—and if computer software is used. Again, some trade-offs may be necessary, depending on the needs, objectives, and resources of your organization.

The Decision to Make or Buy

If your target population is too large to make in-depth interviews practical, or if you have limited resources, you will probably want to use a questionnaire to gather 360° feedback. Once you have decided on this approach, you have two choices available to you: designing one yourself or purchasing one from a vendor who specializes in such instruments.

On the face of it, developing your own customized instrument may seem like a good idea. After all, who understands the needs of your organization better than those inside it? Why pay a vendor to do it when you have the talent right there? Nevertheless, developing a questionnaire in-house can be expensive and time-consuming, and may also increase raters' anxiety about confidentiality.

Fortunately, the guidelines used for selecting an instrument can also help you determine whether to make or buy the questionnaire you will use. Ask yourself the following questions:

- Is your theoretical model of leadership, management, teamwork, or interpersonal effectiveness unique or inconsistent with all the existing models in the literature?

- Do the items on all the questionnaires you have looked at fail to adequately reflect your organization's unique characteristics and needs? Are vendors unable or unwilling to customize the instrument to accommodate your needs?

- Will the data be used to prescribe appropriate behaviors rather than to make people aware of how often they employ certain behaviors?

- Do you have the resources and expertise to develop not only the questionnaire itself but a scoring mechanism to analyze the data and produce a report of the findings (hand-scored or computer-generated) and a complete set of support materials (development guides, participant materials, training program)?

If you have answered "no" to any of these questions, purchasing an instrument may be the best option for you.

Concluding Remarks

Keep in mind that there is no such thing as the perfect instrument for your organization's needs. Some are obviously more thorough and accurate than others, and a few may match up well with your organization's profile and goals. But feedback instruments, no matter how carefully constructed, are necessarily the product of their era and their source. Because change is part of doing business, the social and economic factors affecting the workplace will inevitably vary over time. No instrument can be effective under all conditions. If, however, you have carefully evaluated the available instruments using the criteria described in this chapter, you can be confident that you are using an instrument that is well suited to your purpose.

Chapter Four

Using Interviews to Augment 360° Feedback

One of the best ways to persuade others is with your ears—by listening to them.

—*Dean Rusk*

We have discussed the advantages of using questionnaires to collect 360° feedback in earlier chapters—they are easy to administer, and the clarity and specificity of the quantitative report provide direct messages that can be the catalyst for change. Now, imagine a situation in which you are asked to complete a 360° feedback questionnaire on your boss. You answer each question but are left feeling somewhat dissatisfied. While the questionnaire provides the opportunity to rate how frequently your boss uses certain behaviors and how often you would like him to use them, in the end you feel you have more to say. You would have liked to give examples to help explain why you gave lower ratings on some items, and you wish you could have described when and why some of your boss's other behaviors have had such a positive impact on you personally and on the department overall. You are concerned that your boss will not get the whole picture.

This situation illustrates the limitations of the questionnaire method—it can be difficult to reduce your perceptions of a person's behavior to ratings on a standard set of questions targeted to a general population.

Questionnaire data can be augmented or enhanced in a number of ways—by adding open-ended questions to the questionnaire itself, by administering tests that measure personality or aptitude, or by conducting interviews with direct reports, colleagues, bosses, past associates, friends, and family members. In this chapter, we will discuss the use of interviews to enrich 360° feedback questionnaire data. Topics will include the advantages and disadvantages of using the interview method at various levels of the organization; the planning required to ensure that this approach will be effective; collecting, analyzing, and interpreting the data; and presenting the feedback in a way that maximizes its constructive effects.

Advantages and Disadvantages of the Interview Method

Advantages

Not only can interviewees describe the skills and behaviors they see the manager using, they can also clarify when and why those behaviors are more or less effective and identify themes and patterns of behavior. In addition, they can offer insight into how the manager might change or improve those behaviors to achieve better alignment with business objectives or the organization's culture. A well-run interview will result in anecdotes about specific, critical, on-the-job incidents that can then form the basis for equally specific recommendations for improvement. Says David DeVries of Kaplan DeVries, Inc., "In an interview, if someone says, 'My boss just doesn't appreciate the work I do,' you immediately ask what the person means, and you get an example that you can then cite to the feedback recipient later on. Those examples are often what take the recipient very quickly from a state of bafflement to having to confront the evidence."[1]

This specificity is one of the key advantages of using the interview method. The data that emerge, because they are so directly relevant and clarify what may have seemed like the generic information provided by the questionnaire, are often more likely to have an impact on the recipient; as DeVries points out, it cannot be as easily denied or explained away. Thus, using the interview approach can motivate people to follow through on their development plans with more enthusiasm and commitment than they might otherwise have had.

The interview method also furnishes an opportunity to learn about an individual's temperament and personal characteristics. Interviewees may describe experiences or make observations that shed light on the individual's personality as well as specific skills. Such feedback further enriches and rounds out the picture.

In fact, in some cases, interview data are collected not just from the people with whom the person deals on the job but also from external sources that may include clients as well as the manager's spouse, children, siblings, and close friends. Obviously, interviewing these "significant others" will require a major investment and should be considered only when it seems likely to yield information that is both necessary and unobtainable from other sources.[2]

If resources were not a factor, interviews might always be used to augment questionnaire data. Says Penny Nieroth, president of Learning By Design and a consultant with broad experience in using interviews to augment feedback from questionnaires, "As you establish rapport, people will tell you things at the end of the interview that they would never have told you at the beginning—and that they would certainly never have committed to paper."[3] In addition, according to DeVries, "An added value to interviews is that they can be wonderfully encouraging. When interviewees are asked, 'What else would you like to say to this person?' some powerfully positive words come out."[4]

Given their labor-intensive nature, however, most organizations opt for gathering additional feedback through interviews only when key personnel are involved or when recipients require additional help to decide on development targets and strategies for change.

One way to gain some of the benefits of interviews without incurring the cost is to combine a standardized multiple-choice questionnaire and a separate open-ended questionnaire to which people write in responses. "This approach is more anonymous and quite efficient to score, and we find we get much of the richness of person-to-person interviews," says DeVries.[4]

Disadvantages

For all the advantages to be gained from the interview approach, it does have its drawbacks. We have already mentioned the additional time and money required to conduct the interviews, analyze the data for themes and patterns, and cull the large amount of verbal feedback into a coherent report. While using an internal human resource professional will reduce the costs, most organizations prefer to use outside consultants who are more likely to be experienced at collecting and presenting 360° feedback.

Another potential problem concerns respondents' reluctance to provide in-depth and rich feedback for fear that recipients will be able to identify them from their quotes and examples. Even though they are assured of the anonymity and confidentiality of their feedback, fear of being found out may prevent people from being forthcoming and perfectly honest. For that reason, says DeVries, "the interviewer needs to explain very concretely what is meant by confidentiality and should explain the anonymous form in which the feedback will be presented to the recipient. Explain that you will firmly discourage any speculation about who said what and then follow through on that."[5] To protect the identity of the respondents, we suggest using quotes that reflect the comments of several interviewees. In addition, the quotes selected should not refer to specific situations or information that would enable the recipient to single out any one person. Finally, there is a possibility that a manager who is given both types of feedback at the same time will focus on the written comments from the interview and ignore the quantitative results from the questionnaire.

Ensuring That the Interviews Will Be a Success

Having decided that the interview approach is right for a particular situation, there is a fair amount of work to do before you actually collect the data. The following simple but necessary steps will ensure that the manager you are working with receives the kind of feedback that will add real value.

Clarify the Purpose

To gain commitment to the interview process, it is vital that both recipients and raters understand the purpose of the interview (to clarify questionnaire data, to collect more data, to identify ways to address issues raised in the questionnaire), how it will be conducted, what the results will look like, and how they will be used.

Select the Interviewer-Facilitator

The more the feedback recipient trusts the person who is collecting and analyzing the feedback, the more likely it is that he or she will act on the data collected. Similarly, the more raters trust and "connect" with the interviewer, the more honest and detailed the feedback is likely to be. For that reason, you need to decide at the outset who will be assigned this important role.

You can choose either an internal or an external resource. At first glance, the internal resource may appear to be the more attractive alternative. Not only can you count on an inside person knowing the ins and outs of the organization and its culture, but he or she may already have a relationship with the raters. This instant credibility will mean that they can quickly move beyond the introduction stage. Finally, you can be sure that the internal person will be available for the duration of the project.

However, choosing an external resource has its advantages, too. First, external facilitators are likely to have had more experience at this sort of work. Second, because they are outsiders, they will have no preconceived notions about those who are involved in the process and may be better able to listen without biases or personal opinions. (Often, even a respected internal person will be viewed as more committed to meeting organizational agendas than to helping managers with their development for its own sake.) And finally, when the interviewer is an outsider, both recipients and raters may feel more comfortable being totally candid, since they will not be so worried that their comments might be revealed to others in the organization.

Whomever you choose, you must take into account the skill and credibility of the interviewer. Effective interviewing is both an art and a science, and the ability to elicit information from people that is useful and honest largely depends on:

- *The ability to listen effectively*—to hear both the thoughts and feelings behind the words, to hear what is partially as well as thoroughly articulated, and to probe with questions that draw out specific and relevant information and perspectives without making the interviewee feel defensive.

- *The ability to inspire trust*—to make the interviewees feel relaxed, at ease, and confident of not being either misunderstood or misrepresented; to make people feel that what they are revealing will not be misused. This may be particularly important in the case of direct reports giving feedback to their supervisors. They must have complete trust that what they say will be kept confidential and will have no unpleasant repercussions.

- *The ability to present oneself as a potential source of help and growth*—to be seen as a coach rather than an interrogator, someone who understands all aspects of being an executive and knows what suggestions and recommendations will be perceived as realistic, both during the feedback session and in any follow-up sessions that may take place.

Because it is so vital that the interviewer be trusted and accepted by everyone involved in the process, it is worth spending some time finding the best possible person for the role. You may need to interview several candidates and set up several meetings with the recipient before you find the facilitator who is just right. Remember to make sure, if an external resource is selected, that the person will be available for as long as may be needed to coach the manager through any follow-up activities or next steps.

Whatever time is required to select an interviewer-facilitator is well worth it. A good choice means a strong foundation will have been laid for the rest of the process.

Finalize Objectives and Clarify Deliverables

During this phase of the planning, ask the recipient what he or she would like to get out of the process. This conversation should result in clarifying specific objectives for both the individual and the organization. The participant and the facilitator should decide together who should be interviewed and what type of feedback will be most useful for identifying development goals. Getting participants involved in the planning stages results both in greater commitment to the process and a greater openness to the feedback.

At this stage, you will also want to decide how the feedback should be presented and let the recipient know which method will be used. There are two options, the first of which is a straightforward, one-on-one meeting in which the interviewer and the recipient review the feedback results together, and the recipient identifies a series of appropriate next steps. The second option is to include the manager's boss or a human resource professional who can help define appropriate development goals. Only if the feedback recipient feels comfortable with the idea of having someone else present, however, should this option be chosen.

Whether the feedback is presented one-on-one or with a third party present, we strongly suggest that the report of the findings not be given to the recipient ahead of time to review on his or her own. Even reports that are very positive may contain messages the recipient will find disturbing. An accurate interpretation of the data and an openness to receiving the messages are increased when the first review of the report is conducted by a trusted coach-facilitator.

Develop Interview Questions

Asking the right questions is the most essential ingredient in producing a successful interview. Open-ended questions like, "What do you see as this manager's greatest strength? His greatest weakness? His biggest challenge?" elicit the kind of examples and in-depth analyses that are not forthcoming in any other format. In many instances, follow-up questions prompted by specific (and sometimes unexpected) answers provide further insights that shade, color, and clarify an initial set of responses.

Another effective technique is to ask the recipient of the feedback what questions he or she thinks might produce the most helpful responses. Most people have some sense of where they might need some help, and their suggestions on what to ask often produce the richest answers. Furthermore, they may feel they need clarification of certain data from the questionnaire and want specific questions asked in the interview to help them do that. For that reason, DeVries, among others, always involves the recipient in determining what to ask. As he explains, "Their questions are particularly useful, because people do have an inkling of what their vulnerabilities are."[6]

Below is a list of sample interview questions we have used in the past:

- What is your professional history with the feedback recipient? How long have you known this person and in what capacity?
- Based on your current observations and dealings with this person, how would you say that he or she contributes to the success of the business? What does he or she do that prevents the business from running successfully?
- In today's environment (or given the direction in which the company is headed), what is this person's biggest challenge? What strengths will enable him or her to meet this challenge? What weaknesses might get in the way?

- Describe a time when this person was particularly effective. Describe a time when he or she was particularly ineffective.

- Given the goals of the organization and the environment in which it will operate in the future, what are this person's chief strengths? Weaknesses? What does he or she need to change, improve, or develop to be effective in the future?

- Is there anything you would like to add that you think would help in this person's professional development?

Whatever your final interview format, we recommend learning about both the recipient's behaviors and the context within which he or she works. Of course, you should also use your own experience and knowledge to further focus the questions.

Decide Who Will Be Interviewed

While there may seem to be obvious sources of feedback, such as the individual's boss and direct reports, it is important to consider who would be most likely to have experienced the specific behaviors you are seeking to evaluate. The manager in question is often uniquely qualified to make this judgment. In helping to identify potential raters, the feedback recipient should consider the following questions:

- What are the nature and length of each relationship?
- Has a balance been achieved among peers, direct reports, and bosses? Does it make sense to include former associates and colleagues?
- Who has seen you work under normal circumstances? Special situations?
- Who may have a unique perspective?

If the organization is looking for more in-depth feedback on motivation and personality, as opposed to just information about on-the-job behavior, it might be appropriate to interview the recipient's spouse, family, and close friends. Such interviews can contribute to getting a complete psychological profile of an individual.[7] Because of the time involved and the sensitivity of this type of information, however, it is important to consider whether it is truly likely to help the person achieve specific development goals.

Determine the Interview Format

There are three ways to get your questions answered—telephone interviews, group interviews, and individual, face-to-face interviews. The technique you choose will affect the kind of answers you get. Therefore, it is important to be thoughtful about what format and structure are most appropriate for each case.

Telephone interviews can be quite effective for gathering 360° feedback from a large number of sources who may be scattered in different locations. But however convenient this option may seem, a great deal of subtlety and information can get lost in the translation. Oftentimes, messages of anxiety and frustration will be communicated through simple body language, hand gestures, and facial expressions that go undetected in telephone interviews. Telephone interviews also tend to be shorter because of the physical inconvenience and discomfort of speaking on the phone for long periods. Finally, establishing real trust is more difficult on the telephone.

In our experience, group interviews are the least reliable format. Participants are often unwilling to provide harsh or negative feedback for fear of looking mean-spirited or of being revealed as the source of the critical feedback after the meeting. There are also group dynamics that present a challenge to the interviewer—someone talks too much; someone else does not talk at all. "One thing I've learned," says DeVries, "is never to interview groups. I once interviewed a pair of colleagues. One colleague constantly interrupted and contradicted the other. Then the other colleague would say, 'Yes, that's right. That's what I wanted to say.'"[8]

The most valuable interview format, and the one we have used more than any other, is the individual, face-to-face interview. While this is by far the most time-consuming format, the higher quality of the feedback makes it well worth the investment. Meeting with feedback contributors one-on-one precludes the possibility of group-think and also sends a message to the contributors, especially at the direct report level, that their input is highly valued. The result is a willingness to give specific, thoughtful feedback. Furthermore, the face-to-face interview allows the interviewer to establish rapport and gain the trust and confidence of the feedback giver, who, knowing it will remain anonymous and confidential, provides more honest feedback.

Scheduling Interviews

Whatever format you choose, you will need to schedule interviews with the chosen raters. In the case of individual interviews, we have found it useful for the interviewer(s) to distribute a calendar showing blocks of available time to interviewees, who then indicate which times are their first, second, and third choices. Through a process of elimination, individual interviews can then be scheduled either by an internal resource or directly by the outside consultants. When using outside consultants as interviewers, scheduling the interviews consecutively will save time and money by reducing the number of trips that the consultant must make to the site.

When scheduling the interviews with colleagues, direct reports, and the boss, make sure they are each aware of the hows and the whys of the feedback process. It has been our standard practice to send a confirmation letter either from the interviewer or from the executive describing what will happen in the interview and how long it will last—usually from forty-five minutes to one hour. Included in the confirmation letter is a set of interview questions that will be asked, along with an expression of appreciation for the rater's time and effort and a reaffirmation of the confidentiality of the responses. Including a list of the questions to be asked gets the interviewees thinking about them beforehand, so they come prepared with appropriate anecdotes or examples. Many people also make notes before the interview to be sure that the feedback they give is complete.

The confirmation letters that are sent to each interviewee (by regular mail, e-mail, or fax, depending on the time frame) should include the purpose and the date and time of the interview, as well as the interviewer's name and organization (if applicable) and a telephone number in case of questions or unanticipated scheduling conflicts. An example of an interview confirmation letter follows:

> This is to confirm your interview on Wednesday, July 20 at
> 8:30 A.M. with Bonnie Allyn of Manus, a consulting firm that is
> working with our company to provide individual feedback to each
> member of the Executive Committee.
>
> Manus will be preparing a report for Joan Miller, based
> on interviews conducted with you and several other direct reports
> and colleagues of Joan's. The feedback is designed to help Joan
> identify her strengths and areas for development in order to ensure
> that she is able to provide effective leadership as our company
> moves into a more challenging market environment.
>
> This information will be used only for the purpose of de-
> velopment and will not be seen by anyone else inside the organiza-
> tion. Your individual responses will remain strictly confidential.
>
> The interview should take no more than one hour of your
> time. Among the questions you will be asked are the following:
>
> 1. Describe your relationship with Joan, for example, history,
>   experience, and so forth.
> 2. What do you see as Joan's key strengths as a leader and
>   manager?
> 3. Please think of an example of when you saw these strengths
>   being used. How did they play out? How were you affected?

4. What do you see as Joan's key weaknesses as a leader and a manager?
5. Please think of an example of when these weaknesses were obvious to you. How did they play out? How were you affected?
6. What single area for development would be most important for Joan to attend to, given the direction of the business?
7. Is there anything you would like to add?

Thank you very much for taking the time to provide your feedback. It will be very valuable as Joan plans for her professional development. Please call Manus if you have any questions or scheduling conflicts.

When last-minute scheduling conflicts occur, it is best to reschedule the interview immediately if possible. However, because of time constraints, it may become necessary to compromise, in which case the rater should be given the option of doing the interview on the phone.

Conducting an Effective Interview

To elicit the most useful and comprehensive feedback, the interview should be structured in a way that most nearly reflects the goals of the process. In other words, the interviewer should have a clear sense of how every question and the way it is asked can contribute to achieving the objectives that have been defined. If an organization is concerned about having its managers practice and foster more teamwork, for example, it will not make much sense for the interviewer to ask a lot of questions about the person's performance at essentially solitary pursuits.

If the questions have been prepared and distributed beforehand, is the interviewer's role nothing more than that of a note taker? The answer, very definitely, is "no." By asking for elaboration and examples and by identifying areas for further questioning, the interviewer contributes a great deal to the flow of the session and the quality of the feedback. Following are some tips we have found to be especially effective:

Conduct the interview in a private setting.

Never conduct a face-to-face interview in a common or open area in the workplace. Such a venue makes interviewees reluctant to give honest answers for fear that others will overhear their comments, and the feedback recipient will learn through the grapevine who said what. Conducting the interview in a private, reasonably soundproof room makes people feel more at ease. It also reduces possible distractions, such as a ringing telephone, that could interrupt the discussion.

Be informative.

Although an advance letter may have described the process, be prepared to explain the specific steps you are taking, how the feedback giver will contribute, and what the feedback recipient hopes to learn.

Ensure confidentiality.

Perhaps the single thing most likely to contribute to a successful interview is assuring raters of the absolute confidentiality of their responses. As noted earlier, the interviewer should be very specific and concrete about the steps that are taken to ensure confidentiality and anonymity. Stress that the feedback will be presented to the recipient without any indication of who said what and that the recipient will be actively discouraged from speculating about the source of various comments.

Understand the relationship to the recipient.

All comments must be understood within the context of the history of the relationship between the interviewee and the feedback recipient. This includes both formal and informal roles, shared experiences, and the highs and lows of the relationship over time.

Be flexible.

A good interviewer is prepared with a set of questions but uses them as a springboard for a conversation, not a grilling. The semistructured interview format enables the interviewer to move smoothly from one topic to another, explore and clarify unanticipated responses, and move with the feedback giver's agenda, as well as his or her own. Simply reading a set of questions to the interviewee goes no farther toward gaining an in-depth perspective on the manager's behavior than would a generic survey.

Be responsive.

While listening to detailed descriptions of a person's behavior can be demanding due to the large amount of information to be absorbed, it is important to use verbal and nonverbal prompts and other effective listening techniques to keep the conversation flowing. If an interviewer is trying to write down every word or is sitting in front of a laptop computer typing frantically, interviewees may think he or she is not actually listening to what they are saying. The interviewer must therefore be a good note taker.

If the interviewee is willing, the interviewer might want to bring a colleague to take notes—this will enable the interviewer to concentrate completely on listening and probing for more detail and to respond to and draw out more about the themes and issues that emerge. (This option works best when external resources are being used.) Another option is to ask permission to audiotape the session so that the interviewer can focus completely on the discussion at hand. To set the interviewee at ease, you should explain exactly what will happen to the tape after the session. We frequently offer to provide the interviewee with the tape after it has been transcribed.

Test previous opinions.

The interviewer can use the interview as an opportunity to test whether comments made in previous interviews or the messages culled from a questionnaire are general opinions or the perspective of a single individual. This must be done cautiously and skillfully so as not to lead the respondent or reveal the source of the comments. Feedback givers are often curious to know whether the interviewer has heard this kind of comment before and will look for confirmation.

Go for specifics.

Probing questions should be used to get the details behind an interviewee's initial comments. If, for example, an interviewee says that relations with the recipient are smooth most of the time, the interviewer should ask *when* relations are smooth and also when friction arises. The interviewer should also ask questions that will help clarify why these individuals get along in some situations but not in others, as well as how the interviewee defines friction.

Preparing the Report

Data from face-to-face interviews are typically collected, analyzed, and summarized into themes that are illustrated by verbatim quotations from respondents. When it comes to analyzing and interpreting the feedback, the first thing to do is to look for patterns in the data. How did people describe strengths? How did they describe weaknesses? What sort of examples were provided? Did more than one person observe or comment on the same critical incident? Were there differences of opinion across relationships? Did direct reports, peers, and bosses agree or disagree? To what extent is there consistency among groups of interviewees? Once themes have been established, the next step is to substantiate them with quotes that cite specific behavior. Finally, use the feedback to generate ideas on what possible next steps may be relevant. Describe how the manager's strengths can be leveraged to address weaknesses. It is important to generate these ideas with specific development objectives in mind.

Says Penny Nieroth, "In preparing my report, I always try to organize the data according to a model that is appropriate for what the individual hopes to gain from the process. I also try to emphasize themes that have come up with more than one interviewee. Certain themes and patterns almost always emerge, and the report should be structured around them. The suggestions and recommendations should relate directly—and as concretely as possible—to those themes and patterns."[9]

Sample Interview Feedback Report Format

Excerpts from a selection of reports are given next to show the format, provide a sense of the tone of the report, and illustrate how the themes and quotes work together to create a powerful message.

Feedback Report Prepared for Brandon Campbell

Introduction

Data were collected by conducting eight face-to-face interviews and two telephone interviews with your peers, direct reports, and superiors. The interviews were conducted between December and January. All participants were assured that their comments would be taken in confidence.

This report is organized into three sections. Sections One and Two present the major themes that emerged from the interviews. Representative quotes are provided to elaborate on these themes. Section One focuses on your strengths as seen by others, Section Two reflects areas where development opportunities exist, and Section Three contains ideas on possible actions that might be relevant to your development. This report is intended to be a springboard for discussion and the basis for follow-on meetings to identify next steps and monitor the progress of your development agenda.

Section One: Areas of Strength

Without exception, there was complete agreement on your intellectual suitability for your position. Your problem-solving skills in particular were viewed as extraordinary. Clearly, these abilities should enable you to perform at a high level and to grow within the organization. The following are typical comments:

He is a quick learner and picks up on ideas rapidly.

He can rapidly focus in on and understand the details of a problem.

He has enough of a grasp of technology to successfully apply his problem-solving skills.

He is able to quickly summarize a problem and get to the right questions.

He keeps an open mind when problem solving, is able to quickly prioritize issues, and can juggle a number of problems at once.

Clients, colleagues, and direct reports were also impressed with your ability to channel your problem-solving ability into crisis management.

He is at his best in the middle of a crisis. He keeps his wits and problem solves extraordinarily well.

He is calm and methodical when solving problems, even when the pressures begin to build.

He is able to quickly identify and respond to situations that call for urgent action.

His ability to orchestrate a problem-solving effort maintains itself even as the pressures mount.

Section Two: Areas for Development

One of the basic issues that surfaced related to time management and follow-through. While individuals admired your ability to juggle many balls at once, it was also thought that you could be spread so thin that your ability to follow through on commitments and develop in-depth relationships was inhibited.

He has canceled more than 50 percent of his appointments with me. I know he has to respond to emergencies, but it seems excessive.

He's prone to biting off more than he can chew and getting diluted over too many things. I don't know whether he's doing it to impress management, but it doesn't help in getting the job done.

He is often late to meetings, which is irritating. It generates resentment, and his peers read arrogance into it.

He needs to stay more focused on today.

The management of your relationships was a frequent topic of concern. It was thought that you were less consultative with peers and direct reports than you are with clients. In addition, although direct reports recognize the urgency of addressing client problems, they don't see this as sufficient reason for what they perceive as your lack of availability.

He will spend time with me when there is a problem; otherwise, it is hard to get time with him. As a result, I'm losing the opportunity to grow.

He would do well to get closer to his people and give them the feeling that he would get into the trenches with them.

He should spend more time building trust with people. Sometimes, I get the impression that his ambition comes first, not the people.

If he got to know his people better, including those a couple of layers down, he would build more trust in the department.

Section Three: Possible Next Steps

In general, everyone interviewed perceived you to be a high-potential person with extraordinary problem-solving talents and an openness to self-development. Some of the critical areas for growth will require time and ongoing, conscientious effort to address. The following are some suggestions for your consideration:

- More concentration on the development of people is a crucial component of your development. The most effective leaders are coaches who listen, ask, facilitate, integrate, and provide administrative support. Giving more consideration to individual needs along with department and organizational goals is also in order.
- Time management is another area for development. This is directly tied to your ability to allocate time to furthering the development of direct reports and strengthening your relationships with people, which will also generate a level of trust that would significantly contribute to your long-term effectiveness. The unpredictable nature of the environment in which you work makes this an even more important focus for you.
- Taking action to build a stronger team would be another appropriate goal. You should think about strengthening the elements of teamwork within your group, with particular emphasis on relationships and values.

The order in which this feedback has been presented is not an arbitrary one. To keep the recipient focused and open-minded, we believe the positive feedback should always be presented before the critical feedback. Otherwise, a strong reaction to the criticism may taint the manager's receptiveness to the praise. It is more effective to describe and discuss weaknesses in terms of strengths, rather than vice versa, since it leaves the manager with more optimistic feelings about setting development goals to overcome his or her weaknesses.

The interview feedback should also be presented in behavioral terms. While some raters may have given feedback in personal terms, it is up to the presenter to align the feedback with the behaviors you are seeking to improve.

Presenting the Feedback

There are two segments in a one-on-one feedback session: presenting the feedback report and identifying improvement goals. The presentation may be an anxious time for the recipient, and it is important that the feedback be presented tactfully, yet accurately and forcefully enough to spur further development action. All the effort of the project comes down to this moment, so it is important to maximize its potential.

Keep in mind that the presentation should not be turned into a lecture; rather, it should take the form of a development discussion, with the recipient doing as much of the talking as the presenter. The manager should be encouraged to ask questions and express feelings about the feedback and should then be guided to draw some conclusions about his or her effectiveness. Whether or not that happens is often a function of the presenter's skill. In cases where the recipient is feeling defensive and tries to deny the truth of the messages contained in the feedback, the presenter will need to find ways to overcome that defensiveness and make sure the feedback is heard and accepted.

Agenda for the Feedback Session

The facilitator should present an agenda for the meeting and then ask the recipient how that agenda works for him or her. A sample agenda may look something like the following:

- Set the recipient at ease by asking what he or she is looking forward to in this session and what concerns he or she might have. Establish ground rules and clarify your role.

- Review the strengths from the feedback report.

  Ensure understanding.

  Ask for impressions, reactions.

- Review the weaknesses from the feedback report.

  Ensure understanding.

  Ask for impressions, reactions.

- Review the recommendations from the feedback report.

- Discuss the implications for development.

  Generate ideas together.

  Review strategies for change.

  Determine how the recipient's strengths can be applied to implementing them.

- Choose priorities for development, and discuss how to achieve them. Determine whose support will be required, and establish realistic time frames.

- Establish a time to review how successfully the plan is being implemented.

The Facilitator's Role as Coach

Inevitably, certain recipients will be less receptive to their feedback than others. Particularly in cases where the manager did not volunteer for the process, the presenter may have a difficult time conveying the importance of the feedback for professional development. The facilitator's role then becomes more that of a coach, motivating the executive to take action.

Harold Scharlatt, president of Training and Development Associates, tells of one top-level executive whose first words in his presentation session were, "Don't tell me anything my subordinates said about me, because I'm just not interested." Scharlatt was just as blunt in his response. He said, "My advice is that you'd better begin to care about what they think, because it's going to affect your professional future."[10] It took some time, but the recipient finally began to take his feedback seriously.

Another important person to include in this type of situation is the executive's boss or the individual responsible for initiating the project. This will reinforce the reasons for the feedback and the need for follow-up development. However, keep in mind the confidentiality of the feedback report itself. If including others in the presentation will cause the manager serious discomfort, conduct the feedback presentation alone and then invite others in for a discussion of next steps and development opportunities.

In most cases, the facilitator will be more familiar than anyone else with the manager's feedback and the 360° feedback process. For that reason, it makes sense for him or her to serve as a sideline coach to steer the manager through the development phase. Our experience has shown that feedback is more likely to result in positive behavioral change if a coach is available to help the manager plan development activities, monitor progress, and stay on track. Managers left to their own devices during the creation of the development plan are less likely to take the necessary time to work on it, given that their past behaviors have worked well enough in the past to get them to where they are. In this sense, having a coach becomes essential.

Concluding Remarks

Well-conducted interviews not only provide the richest possible picture of an individual's skills and behavior, they can also be a valuable experience for those providing the feedback. Particularly in cases where the recipient is an important figure to them, interviewees appreciate the chance to clarify their ideas and feelings about the person in a confidential, nonthreatening setting.

The implicit message of every interview should be, "We value your opinion; we really want to hear what you have to say." Creating a positive atmosphere for the interview can lead to more constructive comments and suggestions; raters will see their role as one of providing helpful advice rather than criticism.

Chapter Five

Creating Champions

Selling the Idea to Others in Your Organization

> If you want to persuade people . . . find out what the
> other side really wants and show them how to get it.
> —*Herb Cohen*

While you may feel convinced of the importance of providing people in your organization with multi-source feedback, there are probably other decision makers whose commitment you need to get the process moving. Creating champions of these decision makers and other stakeholders (people who need not actually sign off on the decision but whose commitment is required to implement the process successfully) ensures that the effort will get off to a good start and receive the continued support necessary to sustain it.

In organizations where open and honest multi-source feedback has not been the norm, people's attitudes may be tinged with a fear of the unknown. But if your reasons for wanting to implement a 360° feedback program are the right ones, it should not matter that this is new territory. Although it was once seen as risky, 360° feedback is now widely accepted as an effective method of solving business problems. There is now considerable documentation available that will support your position.

Are You Ready?

Before we discuss how to position the use of multi-source feedback with key decision makers and other stakeholders, let us make sure that you yourself are ready to present it to them.

As you prepare to approach the people whose support you need, you must be sure of both your organization's readiness to use a 360° feedback process and your ability to be an effective advocate. Ask yourself the following questions:

Do you have a clear sense of what 360° feedback is and how it should be implemented? Are you ready to describe the approach and its benefits and to respond to people's questions and concerns?

If not, refer to Chapters One and Six for background on 360° feedback and Chapters Three and Four for an overview of two methods for collecting 360° feedback and guidelines on how to choose an effective approach.

Have you clarified a business need that can be effectively met through the use of 360° feedback? Can you clearly and succinctly articulate this need and explain why multi-source feedback should be considered as part of the solution?

If not, you may want to refer to Chapter Two to see how other organizations have used 360° feedback to resolve business issues.

Can you explain the value of the feedback process to the organization and its individuals and how to ensure that the benefits will be realized long term?

If not, refer to Chapter Eight for guidelines on how to create lasting change through effective follow-up, and Chapter Nine for a discussion of the benefits of using 360° feedback for development, appraisal, and compensation.

Have you thought about how people in the organization will react to the idea of getting 360° feedback? Can you make certain they will get the most out of the experience?

If not, refer to Chapter Seven for a discussion of why people reject feedback and how to present feedback in ways that ensure people will appreciate and act on the messages they receive.

Once you have evaluated your readiness and prepared yourself, your next hurdle will be convincing others in your organization that now is the time and multi-source feedback is the method. In this chapter, we will help you determine how easy it will be for you to create champions, and, once you know what lies ahead, to develop a plan for selling your ideas to the key decision makers whose commitment will be vital to your success.

Objections to Using 360° Feedback

The following arguments against using 360° feedback are those most commonly expressed by key decision makers:

It is not the best use of resources.

We recently spoke with a senior organization development consultant with a company in the Midwest that maintains and provides information on the creditworthiness of individual consumers. The company's senior management team had given him the task of investigating 360° feedback options, ranging from purchasing a commercially developed questionnaire to developing their own questionnaire and processing the reports internally (which was their preferred option). As we discussed the people, dollars, and time required to implement their preferred option, he became very quiet. It seems we had confirmed what he had heard from other sources. "I don't think my boss realized what we'd be committing to by bringing it in-house and doing it all from scratch. I know the senior team is going to have a problem with these numbers." We later found out the project was put on hold.

Every year, organizations engage in the battle of the budget—cutting costs and lowering overhead wherever possible. Each program needs to be justified in terms of productivity and dollars, and to some, the direct and indirect costs of a 360° feedback program seem unjustifiably high. If your organization is considering a standard 360° instrument, the cost per participant can range anywhere from $175 to more than $350. Choosing to design your own instrument increases the costs dramatically, as do one-on-one data-gathering interviews and follow-up training and coaching. Furthermore, administering the process takes precious time.

Your response to this objection should focus on the business need the program will address. With one of our clients, the key to gaining commitment was demonstrating the connection between the feedback process and work unit productivity. You should also be prepared to show how 360° feedback is not only an effective approach to a problem but a cost-effective one as well. As with any long-term investment, you will need to offer evidence that the time and energy devoted to the program will yield results commensurate with the effort. Be open to discussing alternative approaches to addressing the business need before making the case for feedback. In addition, you should be able to discuss the relative costs and benefits of making and buying a 360° feedback system.

It is too risky.

We recently developed a competency model for a firm that was interested in designing a 360° questionnaire to measure how well its top one hundred managers were performing relative to certain key competencies. The competency model was well received, and everyone thought it included the aspects of the job that were most essential to effectiveness. But the 360° feedback project never got off the ground. Senior managers were uneasy about rating and evaluating the behavior of their peers and direct reports. As one of them said, "How honest can I be? I've got to work with these guys tomorrow." They also felt that communicating the behaviors in the competency model would create an expectation within the organization that top managers would conduct themselves according to the values and principles embedded in the model. Senior management just was not sure they were ready to make that commitment.

This sense of the risk involved is common in organizations unfamiliar with 360° feedback. Some decision makers are concerned that a 360° feedback process will make everyone uncomfortable and create rifts in working relationships, thereby negatively affecting productivity. Others fear that the process could lead to unrealistic expectations of organizational or individual change. In that sense, they see 360° feedback as an implicit promise, and they do not want to promise anything they are not sure they can deliver.

Your response to this objection should focus on the link between the behaviors that are being measured and organizational effectiveness. This is an opportunity to position 360° feedback as the foundation of a constructive, up-front conversation about the extent to which the behaviors that contribute to organizational success are being used. To overcome this concern, you must be able to demonstrate that it will be riskier not to take action—that, in the long term, leaving these things unsaid and unexplored will place the company's future in jeopardy.

It is too time-consuming and distracting.

Every year or so, we get a call from the vice president of human resources of a very successful consumer products company to discuss using 360° feedback to ensure that people have the skills they need to work effectively in teams. Because the business has been experiencing rapid growth, their existing organizational structure, which worked well when revenues were one-third of what they are today, is being strained to the limit. Cross-functional communication and teamwork are becoming increasingly necessary as they try to maintain their extraordinary growth rates. Each time, unfortunately, senior management rejects the proposal, although they acknowledge the value and appropriateness of the idea (that must be what encourages her to try again periodically). But they feel that focusing on team development would be a diversion and cause them to "take their eyes off the ball." As they see it, they do not have time to solve the problem; instead, they hope that sooner or later it will go away.

While it may take only twenty to thirty minutes for one rater or recipient to complete a questionnaire, the total time required is quite significant. Interviews are even more time-consuming, lasting from one to three hours each. Then there is the time required to administer the process, present the feedback, and create development plans. All this is downtime for other activities.

Your response to this objection should focus on the opportunity cost and the value of addressing the problem in a proactive manner. In a competitive environment that requires quick responses to changes in the marketplace and the moves of competitors, an organization that is not functioning at peak efficiency will get left behind. Although it may be true that the problem will fix itself over time, can the organization afford to let the solution evolve? Helping the decision makers see that any short-term downtime will be an investment in the long-term effectiveness of the organization will help get your proposal serious consideration. Another approach is to start small: give people a chance to see the benefits of a 360° feedback program without asking for major commitments of time and money. Those who participate in the initial offering are likely to become strong advocates for increasing the scope of the effort.

It will not make any difference.

When we were meeting with the vice president of a multinational chemical company to discuss the use of a 360° questionnaire as part of a leadership development program for his organization, we were surprised to hear him say, "I don't think people are going to pay attention to what their direct reports or colleagues say about them anyway, so why bother?" He added that he did not see the connection between the feedback process and his work unit's performance. "How will this help me hit my third-quarter targets?" was a comment he would use from time to time during our discussion.

Many line managers are skeptical of the business value of feedback and fail to see how it can possibly be relevant to meeting organizational goals. Unfortunately, their skepticism can become a self-fulfilling prophecy, since without their support the feedback process is unlikely to have the impact it has in organizations committed to the effort.

Confronted with this type of objection, you should start by getting the decision maker's agreement that certain behaviors are indeed critical to the organization's effectiveness. For example, if cross-functional cooperation will get the next product to the market faster, you can then describe how 360° feedback can be used as an opportunity to shape people's behavior by communicating what is expected, establishing standards of performance, and monitoring the use of effective teamwork. Your argument should also focus on the value of seeing yourself as others see you and the positive impact this has on work relationships and work unit effectiveness. Your ability to make a strong connection (using real examples from the decision maker's experience) between the feedback, individual and team effectiveness, and work unit performance will help overcome this objection.

Things are fine, so why bother?

The vice president of training and development for a privately held cosmetics company once asked us to work with them to develop a management training program that would include a 360° feedback questionnaire. A few days later, after the company had announced a very successful initial public offering (IPO), we got a call from our client explaining that the management development initiative had been canceled. It turned out that senior management did not want to allocate the funds. The reason they gave was that the company must be well managed already, since the IPO had been so successful. So, the logic went, why devote time and money that could be used elsewhere to train managers who were obviously doing just fine?

This is a fairly common feeling in organizations that are experiencing growth and success. Summed up in the saying, "If it ain't broke, don't fix it," the feeling is based on the notion that development programs are necessary only when problems are interfering with current profitability.

Your response to this objection should focus on two issues. The first is external benchmarks. Companies that measure themselves against internal indicators of their own performance may appear to be doing very well. This picture may not hold up when the company is measured against the performance of its peer group for these indicators. The second point to be made relates to the wisdom of not waiting for a problem to be serious before taking action. You should use critical incidents to illustrate a potential problem that is not yet serious and discuss the value of preventive action.

Jay Strunk, manager of training and development for Zeneca Pharmaceuticals, recalls his experience of trying to implement the idea of using 360° feedback in his organization. "There always have been and always will be people who resist, people who just don't want it. But when we put improvement teams together, people from all parts of the organization began telling senior management what would make for a better organization, and one of the things they recommended was a feedback instrument. Because of senior management's strong commitment to continuous improvement, they got behind the effort. The way work is approached here is to tie everything to the goals of the organization. Of course there are egos here, there is defensiveness here, but there is also a strong commitment to helping everyone develop to their fullest capacity. At the end of the day, it wasn't about 360° feedback; it was about how to achieve higher performance. So the improvement teams' recommendations carried the day."[1]

Strunk's experiences at Zeneca illustrate two important points about gaining commitment for a 360° feedback instrument. First, it is key that the feedback process be seen as an integral part of achieving organizational goals. Second, having senior management behind the process goes a long way toward overcoming people's objections. Your strategy for creating champions, therefore, should address both those issues.

Degrees of Support

Before you begin your campaign, you need to be aware that not all attempts to gain the support of key individuals will result in total commitment. There are three possible levels of support you can expect to achieve. They are:

Commitment. You are most successful if the decision maker or stakeholder agrees with the action or decision you are taking and is proactive in supporting the initiative. Indications of commitment on the part of a decision maker could include agreeing to fund the effort, using his or her group for a pilot, and actively working to gain the support of other key people.

Compliance. You are partially successful if the decision maker or stakeholder agrees with the idea but makes only a lukewarm effort to support it. Indications of compliance might include not trying to block the effort but not actively enlisting the support of others, sending a few direct reports to a pilot program but not attending it personally, and acting on your requests in a timely manner but only doing exactly what was asked, without initiating any activity that supports the effort. Of course, in some cases compliance is all that is required (for example, when a specific stakeholder is not required to take any action, but a general consensus among all stakeholders is desirable). However, if fuller participation is required later, you will probably need to move the person from compliance to commitment.

Resistance. You are unsuccessful if the decision maker or stakeholder is opposed to your request or plan and actively avoids supporting it. Indications of resistance include seeking to have the proposal nullified, arguing against it, or delaying action on it. In the worst case, a key individual may pretend to comply but will try to undermine the effort.

As you will probably have realized, it is much easier to gain people's compliance than to secure their enthusiastic commitment. However, if you want to ensure the success of the 360° feedback effort, full commitment will be required from as many key people as possible. Without it, they will have little success convincing others in the organization of the worthiness of the effort, nor will they be willing to support it energetically over time.

Do Your Homework

Even when a 360° feedback program is supported in the human resource area, staff and line managers are likely to perceive it as too "touchy-feely" or as a waste of valuable time and money. However, to ensure that the program is implemented successfully, you will need the support of these managers throughout the company. Creating champions among this pragmatic group is best accomplished by addressing their concerns, getting their input on the objectives and goals of the effort, and involving them in the planning and implementation process.

The better prepared you are, the more likely it is that you will be able to convince others that 360° feedback is a viable solution to the need or problem you have identified. Two types of preparation are essential if you want to win. The first, as we have noted, is related to knowledge of the subject—you must be able to anticipate and answer questions about the use of 360° feedback and explain how it will meet the needs of the business. The second type of preparation relates to each decision maker's position on the subject of 360° feedback. Is he or she receptive to the idea, and if not, what contributes to the lack of enthusiasm?

Before you can create an effective action plan for turning key individuals into advocates, you will need to decide exactly whose support will be vital to the effort and try to anticipate their reactions to the proposal. A step-by-step process for identifying and analyzing key decision makers and stakeholders is described next.

Identify Key Decision Makers and Other Stakeholders

The easiest way to identify your stakeholders is to construct a Stake-holder Map.[2] You can do this alone, but you will get better results if you enlist the aid of colleagues who are involved with you in the 360° feedback project.

Step 1. List all the people who need to approve the decision, and then list all the individuals and groups you can think of who might (1) benefit, (2) be negatively affected, or (3) be inconvenienced by what you are doing.

Do not overlook members of your own team. Look for "hidden stakeholders"—usually individuals who have personal reasons for not wanting a particular initiative to be implemented. Follow the rules of brainstorming for this step.

Step 2. Categorize the decision makers and stakeholders you iden-tified in Step 1 as *positive* or highly committed to the idea (+), *neutral* or willing to comply but not likely to be active advocates (0), *negative* or likely to resist the idea and oppose it (–), or *don't know* (?). Try to put yourself in each stakeholder's shoes and view the idea from his or her perspective.

Step 3. Now, draw a Stakeholder Map similar to the one in Exhibit 5.1. Put circles around stakeholders likely to support your effort, tri-angles around stakeholders who will comply but not actively sup-port, squares around stakeholders likely to resist, and nothing around stakeholders you cannot categorize until you collect more informa-tion. Put the most important stakeholders—those with the most in-fluence over your success or failure—close to the center of your map. Continue to collect the information you need to complete your map, and update it as you learn more about your stakeholders.

Your next task is to analyze your stakeholders. As a result of your mapping activity, you have identified all the important stakeholders

Exhibit 5.1. Stakeholder Map

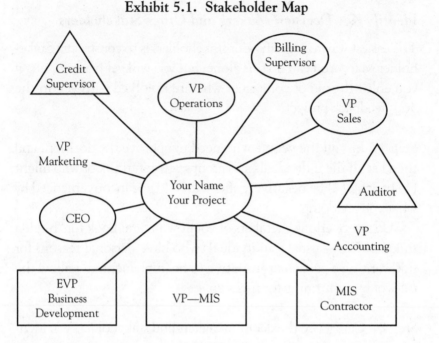

and categorized them according to how they will react to your proposal. Before you develop a plan for influencing them, it is important
to know what each stakeholder stands to gain or lose if your effort is
successful.

Each stakeholder, whether an individual or a group, will view
your effort both from an organizational and a personal perspective.
To better anticipate how they will react to your proposal, answer
the following questions from each stakeholder's point of view:

*Does this project serve the interests of my work unit (the part of the orga-
nization with which I identify most closely)?*

How might this project affect me personally?

Causes of Lack of Commitment

Now that you have clarified who the key stakeholders are and the degree of support you can expect from each, you need to focus on those

stakeholders who you believe will resist the idea of using 360° feedback and those whose commitment is required but from whom you can expect only compliance. Begin by clarifying the possible reasons for these people's lack of commitment. Common reasons include:

The purpose of using multi-source feedback is not made clear.

When people lack a full understanding of how the multi-source feedback will be used, anxiety, rumors, and suspicion usually fill the vacuum. What exactly is the business problem or opportunity this proposal is trying to address?

Effective communication is the most powerful tool for eliminating this type of resistance and building support. Whether your 360° feedback process is a major organizational intervention or a modest effort involving just a few people, you can never communicate too much or too often. When one of our clients decided to use 360° feedback as part of a leadership development and culture change initiative, the CEO held a series of meetings with senior people across the organization to explain why the project was important and what the expected benefits to the company were. In addition, a senior manager kicked off each session, answered questions about the business's performance, and discussed why the 360° feedback effort was necessary and timely. After these meetings, the level of enthusiasm for the project was appreciably higher across the board.

People are not involved in the planning.

When stakeholders feel their input has not been taken into account in planning the feedback process, they are much more likely to resist it. Partly, this is because it is human nature for people to support what they help to create. But apart from any ego issues involved, people want to be sure their issues and needs will be fully addressed before they will make the effort required to ensure the success of the process.

The most straightforward way to address this issue is to treat decision makers and other stakeholders as clients or customers. This means taking time to understand their needs and involving them from the earliest stages of the decision-making process. We suggest getting all stakeholders involved in the clarification of the business need, the identification of the behaviors on which to give feedback, and the decision on which method will be used to collect the data. You should also get their ideas on how to overcome any obstacles they believe may stand in the way of successful implementation. We have found that a task force or temporary committee works well as a vehicle to ensure the involvement of key individuals and build consensus.

Gail Howard, at UJB Financial (now Summit Bank), used a task force to build a coalition of support and ensure that the needs of key people were always at the forefront of discussions and planning. At the earliest stages of the project, Howard assembled twenty of the most competent and respected managers from around the company. She made sure each function and line of business was represented, as well as field personnel. The task force was involved in determining the specific objectives of the project, identifying the competencies required for effective performance of the jobs under consideration, selecting vendors to support the task force's work, and developing and monitoring implementation plans. The high degree of participation actually saved time and allowed the project to move along smoothly and on schedule. Problems and concerns were identified and resolved early, so there were fewer false starts and less need to revisit decisions and resell ideas.

Negative Perceptions of Multi-source Feedback

If previous efforts to use 360° feedback in the organization have had a negative effect, your efforts will probably meet with resistance. Examples of negative effects include 360° feedback being used inappropriately, the stakeholder receiving negative feedback in an ineffective manner without support or facilitation to ensure understanding, or a stakeholder's contributing honest feedback and being punished for doing so.

In this case, you must first clarify the cause of the negative perception. Is it based on first-hand experience, or is it a general impression? If the former, you can explain the strategies in place for ensuring that the problems concerning the stakeholder will be prevented from recurring; you can also ask for further suggestions on how to achieve this. If the negative perception stems from a general impression not based on personal experience, the best way to change the person's mind is to let him or her experience the process in a way that is perceived to be risk free.

When we encountered resistance among members of a task force that was helping to plan the implementation of a 360° feedback process in a large chemicals company, we were confused. We had been working with them for a number of weeks to identify the key behaviors to be measured, and they had seemed enthusiastic and committed. But as we approached the phase of the project that involved actually using feedback, the group began raising questions about potential negative effects on recipients' motivation and the problems associated with completing questionnaires honestly and accurately. As the discussion continued, it dawned on us that a lack of first-hand experience was at the root of their concerns. It turned out that only two of the fifteen members of the task force had ever received or provided 360° feedback. Our solution was to make the task force our pilot group. Once they experienced the process themselves, their anxiety and suspicion were converted into enthusiastic support.

Concerns About How the Feedback Will Be Used

Selling the idea of using 360° feedback for appraisal or compensation can be more difficult than proposing its use for development purposes only. Stakeholders may not want to be held accountable for any potential problems that could arise as a result of an improperly used feedback process.

We recommend that, to start with, 360° feedback be used for development only, particularly if this is the organization's first experience with it. There is less risk associated with this approach, especially since individuals have more control of the data and how they are used. It also provides them with experience using multisource feedback and helps them understand how it could contribute to other human resource management systems. If, however, the feedback is intended for use in appraisal and compensation systems, the focus of your conversation should be on the steps you have taken to ensure the integrity and accuracy of the data that will be collected.

Overcoming Resistance

Once you have identified each stakeholder's most likely cause of resistance, you are ready to approach the individuals on your map. The chart in Exhibit 5.2 summarizes the causes of resistance and lack of commitment, as well as recommended actions to address each.

Developing a Plan of Approach

Before you approach key decision makers, you should be clear about what you hope to achieve. How will you know when you have gained commitment? What exactly do you want this person to do? Once you have made those determinations, using the analysis of resistance and its causes, flesh out your plan using a template similar to the following:

1. Name a decision maker or stakeholder.
2. Consider what you want this person to do—lend the use of a name, champion actively, provide funding?
3. Consider what this person's goals, values, and needs are.
4. Consider what concerns this person might have that would lead to resistance.
5. Determine what actions can be taken to address those concerns.

Exhibit 5.2. Stakeholders' Causes
of Resistance and Recommended Actions

Cause of Resistance	Recommended Actions
The purpose of multi-source feedback is not made clear.	Hold an informal discussion with individuals to review the reasons for the feedback process and to answer any questions.
	Link feedback to the attainment of organizational goals, while also explaining how people would benefit personally.
	Ask for situations in their units where 360° feedback would add value.
People are not involved in the planning.	Encourage participation whenever possible.
	Present your implementation plan as tentative, and solicit advice and suggestions on how to make the program as effective as possible.
	Use a task force that is made up of credible people who represent various work units.
People have negative perceptions of 360° feedback.	Make clear why and how this effort will be different.
	Solicit suggestions on how the problems people experienced in the past can be avoided.
	Get people to experience the feedback process as it will be used in your organization, and give them the chance to evaluate it for themselves.
People are concerned about how the feedback will be used.	Begin by using 360° feedback for development alone.
	Describe how the accuracy of the data and the integrity of the process will be assured.
	Give people control over their feedback.

6. Clarify what this person would see as the benefit of the proposal. Consider both organizational and personal benefits.

7. Consider possible objections this person may raise during the discussion. How will you respond to each objection?

8. Determine the type of approach that is likely to work best with this person—fact-based, value-based, participative, or collaborative.

9. Decide how you will begin the conversation. What will your opening remarks be?

10. Think about what will make the conversation easy.

11. Think about what will make the conversation difficult. What can you do to lessen the difficulty?

As you put your plan into action, you can increase the likelihood that you will achieve your objective if you follow these guidelines:

1. Use your past experiences with this person to identify the approach that is likely to be most effective.

2. Anticipate objections, and be prepared to answer any questions or concerns with well-thought-out responses.

3. Listen carefully. Show you are listening by paraphrasing what has been said, then directly address the stakeholder's issues or concerns in your answer.

4. Be flexible. Be willing to address problems and incorporate others' suggestions and concerns into your future planning.

Concluding Remarks

When you first begin analyzing your situation and determining what it will take to gain people's commitment, you may want to keep these questions and checklists close at hand. You may even find it useful to put your plans of approach on paper. However, as you become more experienced at creating champions, you will find you have internalized the advice given in this chapter, until it has become almost second nature. Instead of mapping out your discussions in laborious detail, you will be able to plan for them while you are driving your car or even during the meetings themselves. You may also find that the general techniques described here are helpful in a broad range of situations. Certainly, you should find them useful during the implementation phase of the 360° feedback effort, when other groups and individuals will need to be won over.

Part Two

Implementing a
360° Feedback System

Chapter Six

Gathering the Feedback

Tips on Administering the 360° Process

It is best to do things systematically, since we are
only human, and disorder is our worst enemy.

—Hesiod

Once you have decided which 360° feedback method to use—questionnaires, interviews, or a combination of the two—you will need to think about how to administer the process efficiently and with the least disruption to your organization. This is an important consideration, although many organizations do not give it much thought until they have actually embarked on the process. The success of the feedback program, the quality of the feedback, and participants' motivation to translate their data into action will depend on the extent to which everyone understands what to do, how to do it, and when to do it.

Planning

Administering 360° feedback successfully requires intelligence and organization. Some critical issues that need to be considered and planned for early in the process include:

How will people be informed that they will be participating in a 360° feedback process?

Although you have been immersed in the 360° process—getting commitment from key decision makers, selecting an approach—

many people in the company will not know anything about this effort, its purpose, or what will be expected of them. To ensure their enthusiastic participation, individual concerns will have to be addressed, expectations will have to be clarified, and the steps of the data collection process and people's role in it will have to be explained.

How will raters be chosen? How many people should complete question-naires or participate in interviews?

Rater selection is a critical component of the 360° process, since perceptions about the source of feedback largely determine how receptive the subjects of that feedback will be. Unfortunately, however, recipients often do not consider this factor until they are looking at their results and questioning whether the people who rated them really provided unbiased and useful information.

A selection method that is advocated by most experts in the field is to have participants choose their own raters, according to a specific set of criteria. This gives feedback recipients a sense of having ownership of the process and therefore makes it more likely that they will focus on getting meaning out of their data rather than rationalizing them.

How can we ensure the anonymity of the raters and the confidentiality of the responses?

Raters are more comfortable providing honest and candid feedback anonymously, since they do not want to compromise their working relationship with the employee when it is necessary to give negative feedback; this is even more true when the rater is a direct report who is providing feedback on his or her boss. Ensuring anonymity reduces the likelihood that the feedback recipient will confront any one rater individually and put that person on the spot about negative comments.

When 360° feedback is new to an organization, people may have questions about the confidentiality of the data and how they will be used. If managers believe their data will be part of their performance appraisal or will influence a promotion or salary decision, they are more likely to rationalize the feedback and put the most positive spin on it. People need to be assured that the data are for their personal and professional development and that their individual reports will not be shared with anyone else in the organization without their consent.

If aggregate, organization-level data have been compiled, people should have the opportunity to review those data and compare their own results to the composite. They should also have information about how the composite data will be used.

How can we ensure that people are not asked to complete too many questionnaires or participate in too many interviews?

Receiving too many questionnaires to complete for other people or being asked to schedule time for multiple interviews can diminish people's enthusiasm for the project and result in poor-quality feedback. Organizations in which large numbers of people are involved in the feedback effort can avoid this problem by setting guidelines for the maximum number of times any one rater has to provide feedback. Making sure that people do not receive more than three questionnaires or participate in more than two interviews during a given period of time is a straightforward solution.

How can we monitor questionnaires that are returned for processing? What can we do to ensure that each person gets enough responses to make for a meaningful feedback report without violating confidentiality or anonymity?

To protect the confidentiality and anonymity of raters and ensure high-quality data, most 360° feedback systems require that a minimum number of questionnaires be returned before a feedback report is produced. With hundreds of questionnaires being sent out and returned, keeping tabs on them all can be difficult. It is essential, however, to keep track of those still outstanding and to find a way of getting them back. This is an essential clerical task and one often performed by the vendor. In this chapter, we will share with you what we, our colleagues, and our clients have learned about how to administer 360° feedback processes successfully.

Introducing the Feedback Process

The ideal method for introducing and explaining the feedback process to your target population is to hold one-on-one or group orientation sessions for participants. Depending on the number of participants involved and how comfortable they are with the concept of 360° feedback, these sessions could range in duration from one hour to a half-day. Another option for introducing people to the 360° effort is with a letter.

Group Orientation Meetings

At UJB Financial (now Summit Bank), where participants new to the process initially felt a high level of discomfort, half-day group meetings were led by experienced facilitators. Employees learned about the process and were encouraged to ask questions and discuss their concerns. This gave the facilitators an opportunity to address and overcome any resistance at the outset.

At these meetings, guidelines were established for how many questionnaires any one person should be expected to complete (three). In a particularly valuable part of the session, participants filled out their own self-report questionnaires. This gave the process immediate momentum and also enabled participants to become familiar with the content of the questionnaire, putting them in a better position to identify potential raters. Finally, participants were coached on how to ask potential raters for their feedback.

The sessions, which were a great success, were seen as a critical factor in the participants' subsequent commitment to the 360° feedback process. In applications of a smaller scale, organizations can take advantage of regularly scheduled staff meetings to achieve similar objectives. A complete outline of the group orientation meeting follows.

Group Orientation Meeting Outline

I. Explain the purpose of the effort.
   A. Link it to a strategic or business objective.
   B. Describe how the feedback will be used.
II. Demonstrate support from senior management.
   A. Have a senior executive as keynote speaker for the orientation session, or . . .
   B. Distribute a letter to participants from the CEO or president emphasizing the importance of the effort, or . . .
   C. Explain the extent to which senior management has been involved in the process, that is, received the feedback themselves.
III. Explain the 360° feedback process in detail.
   A. Provide an overview of the 360° feedback process.
      1. Explain how it will work.
      2. Review the time frame and deadlines.
   B. Introduce internal personnel who will be coordinating the effort.
   C. Distribute questionnaire packets to participants.
   D. Take a packet apart and review its contents.
      1. Explain what the various boxes on the answer sheets are for.
      2. Identify and explain what the machine-readable codes on the answer sheets are for.
      3. Explain how the questionnaires are processed and scored.

    E. Discuss the criteria and process for rater selection.
       1. Stress rater anonymity and the confidentiality of the feedback.
       2. Review the process for distributing packets to raters.
    F. Review the process for returning the completed questionnaires.
    G. Demonstrate how to complete the self-report.
    H. Have participants complete their self-reports.
    I. Collect completed self-reports.
IV. Describe follow-up development programs and activities.
V. Field questions and concerns; check for understanding.

One-on-one Orientation Meetings

When a large Southeastern utility decided to use 360° feedback as part of its effort to encourage teamwork and cross-functional collaboration among members of its senior management team, it took a slightly different, more individualized approach. Since these senior executives had participated in the decision to use 360° feedback, they were already aware that it was going to happen. However, the details of the feedback process still needed to be communicated and explained: What would happen during the process? How would it happen? What criteria should they use to select raters? And a reminder was needed about why it was important.

To do this most effectively, we recommended that one-on-one meetings be held. Beforehand, a letter should be sent to each person providing a brief overview of the process and mentioning that an outside consultant would be contacting him or her to schedule a face-to-face meeting. In the case we are describing, after scheduling a convenient time, we met with each executive individually. We began each meeting by reviewing the purpose of the effort and how it tied in with the organization's business goals. To emphasize both the importance of the program and senior management's commitment to it, we explained that the executive committee members had already gone through the feedback process themselves. We then explained how the feedback was going to be gathered using questionnaires and interviews and who it would be gathered from, stressing that the process would be conducted confidentially and that all responses would remain anonymous.

We also asked each executive to identify, based on the goals and development needs discussed, five raters he or she wanted us to interview. Because we were keeping a master list of who was being interviewed, managers were told if someone they had selected had already been chosen by two other participants. In some cases, we asked the manager to identify another source. In other cases, we left it up to the raters themselves to decide if they would be willing to provide feedback on all the people who had asked them for it. We closed each meeting by explaining that after collecting and analyzing their feedback, we would meet with them again to help plan for their professional development.

In addition to providing a highly effective, personalized method for introducing and explaining the feedback process, these meetings also gave participants an opportunity to clarify their goals and expectations in a one-on-one setting. As a result, we were able to obtain a further level of commitment.

A detailed outline of the one-on-one orientation is provided below.

One-on-one Orientation Meeting Format

I.   Explain the purpose of the effort.
   A. Describe the link to the business strategy or objective.
   B. Clarify how the feedback will be used.
   C. Review the participant's role in this process.
II. Demonstrate the commitment of senior management.
   A. Review how others in the organization have already participated in the effort.
   B. Relay the experiences of senior management (with their permission) that illustrate the benefits of the process.

III. Explain the 360° process in detail.
  A. Review the model of leadership and management on which the questionnaire or interview questions are based.
  B. Describe the process of administering the questionnaire.
  C. Describe the interview process and the value of this approach.
  D. Describe how data from both methods will be integrated and presented.
  E. Discuss criteria for selecting raters, and ask the participant to identify potential raters.
IV. Describe follow-up activities.
V. Close by addressing any remaining questions and concerns.

Introductory Letters

Facilitated approaches such as the ones we have described may be too time-consuming for many organizations, especially if the target population is large. An alternative approach that is especially appropriate for organizations experienced with feedback systems, or where there are few issues around giving or receiving feedback, is to send participants a letter explaining the process. Sample letters to both participating employees (ratees) and raters are provided below:

Sample Cover Letter and Instructions

We are pleased that you are joining the thousands of managers who have used Compass: The Managerial Practices Survey to help them understand their leadership effectiveness. Compass will help you gather information from your direct reports, colleagues, and boss. This feedback will be displayed in a confidential report prepared for you.

All the information and directions people will need to complete the answer sheets are included in the questionnaire booklets. You may want to include a cover letter asking people to fill out the questionnaire and to return it promptly. Attached is a sample cover letter; please feel free to use or adapt it if you wish.

Please use the guidelines below to distribute the attached questionnaires immediately:

Instructions

Step 1: Complete the Self-Report.

Complete your Self-Report questionnaire.

Return your completed Self-Report answer sheet to us, along with the questionnaire booklet, in the enclosed envelope.

Step 2: Choose People to Provide Feedback.

When choosing people to provide you with feedback, select people you deal with frequently and with whom you have worked for at least four months. You have several options. You can distribute the questionnaires to:

- Direct reports only (people who report directly to you)
- Colleagues only (people you work with but have no direct authority over—peers, members of a project team, and so forth)
- A combination of direct reports and colleagues

Step 3: Distribute Importance Questionnaire.

Place the blue Importance Questionnaire in the unsealed Importance Questionnaire envelope.

Give this envelope to your boss.

Step 4: Distribute Direct Report/Colleague Questionnaire Booklets and Answer Sheets.

Place each Direct Report/Colleague answer sheet, together with a Direct Report/Colleague questionnaire booklet, in an unsealed Direct Report/Colleague envelope.

Distribute these eight envelopes to direct reports and/or colleagues, taking care to distribute them according to the relationship you marked on the Self-Report answer sheet.

Sample Cover Letter to Accompany Questionnaire

Dear _____:

In the near future, I'll be attending a professional development
program. As a part of this program, I'll be looking at my leadership
strengths and at how I can do my job more effectively. I need your
help to get an accurate picture of my current behavior on the job.

Enclosed you'll find a copy of Compass: The Managerial
Practices Survey. Could you please complete it by the date specified and mail the questionnaire answer sheet, along with the booklet, in the envelope provided?

Please be sure to answer all the questions as honestly and
accurately as possible—all data received by Manus are kept strictly
confidential. Since I will receive only a composite of the responses
showing how the combined group of people responded, I will not
be able to identify who said what.

Thank you for providing me with valuable and honest
feedback.

Sincerely,

Selecting Raters

Various research studies indicate that, as noted above, the source of
the feedback is often the most important factor in determining
whether the recipient accepts or rejects it. The critical characteristic of a reliable source is credibility, which is based on two key attributes—expertise and trustworthiness. The recipient must believe
the rater is familiar enough with the task, and with his or her performance of the task, to make an accurate judgment. The recipient
must also trust the source's motives—is the feedback intended to be
constructive, or does the rater have an ax to grind? Are the recipi-

ent and the rater in some sense competitors? In general, the more a recipient believes in raters' credibility, the more likely it is that he or she will accept the feedback and use it to change.[1]

For that reason, involving people in the decision about who provides feedback and spending time helping them make the best choices will have a tremendous pay-off later on. As one manager said after he looked at his feedback report, "If I had known how useful this was going to be, I would have been much more careful about choosing people to complete the questionnaires."

Guidelines for Selecting Raters

To aid participants in making the best possible choice of raters, explain that they should focus on potential raters' history and experience with them and offer the following guidelines:

- Has this person worked with you long enough to have observed you in a variety of situations?
- Do you depend on this person to get work done now?
- Will you feel comfortable discussing your key learnings from the feedback with this person—will he or she be willing to engage in honest, reflective conversation about it?
- Does this person understand the nature of your work and the challenges and opportunities you face?

Suggest that they narrow the pool of raters by selecting people

- From various rater groups with a variety of perspectives (for example, colleagues, boss, direct reports, internal customers, external customers). They should choose no fewer than three (except for their boss) from each group to ensure anonymity.
- With whom they have a range of relationships: some with whom they get along well and some with whom they don't get along so well.

While many organizations allow feedback recipients to choose their own raters, some prefer to preselect respondents to ensure an unbiased and representative distribution. Digital Equipment Corporation, for example, randomly selects raters from the employee's work group using a computer-generated system, and raters are then notified via e-mail that they have been chosen to participate.[2]

Preselection of respondents can, however, make participants feel that they have less control over the process, which decreases their commitment and the likelihood that they will accept their feedback and feel motivated to change. While allowing people to choose their own respondents can sometimes mean participants will distribute questionnaires only to their friends, if the feedback is confidential, even friends will usually provide honest responses that indicate where improvement is needed.

How Many Sources of Feedback Are Enough?

Regardless of who selects the raters, we recommend setting minimum and maximum limits for how many are chosen. These limits depend on the importance of rater anonymity to the organization and on the kind of time and resources it is willing to devote to administering the process. In most companies, a minimum of three people from any single rater group (such as direct reports or colleagues) and a maximum of ten feedback givers is ideal. With this minimum, individual raters' responses will be more difficult to identify than if only one or two raters were allowed; it also ensures an adequate sample size. Setting limits on the number of raters ensures that administration will be manageable, since more raters mean more time spent on keeping track of each participant's feedback. Failure to limit raters to a manageable number also increases the likelihood that any one individual will be hit with multiple requests for feedback, which can result in low commitment and less accurate data.

Who Should Provide Feedback?

In addition to the individual's self-ratings, 360° feedback usually includes data from a manager's boss, peers, and direct reports, with customers inside and outside the business sometimes asked to participate. Where "enhanced" 360° feedback is the chosen approach, data are gathered not only from these sources but also from the person's family members and friends, psychological profiles, early work history, and childhood experiences.[3]

Customer feedback is widely regarded as extremely valuable and powerful, since the customer's perceptions and expectations are of key importance for many organizations. However, eliciting customer feedback can lead to a number of administrative problems. For example, since the behavior an external customer has a chance to observe may be different and more limited than that seen by the person's immediate coworkers, different questions are needed, and the resulting data have to be compiled and presented separately. There is also a risk that the customer will perceive requests for feedback as onerous, time-consuming, and disruptive to his or her business, especially if the request is not made tactfully, or the benefits to the customer are not made clear.

Because raters will be providing feedback on what they have observed about a person's behavior, their data will be more accurate and appropriate if they have worked with that person for a reasonably long time. Therefore, it is a good idea to require that each rater have worked with the recipient for at least four to five months.

Rater Anonymity

The issue of rater anonymity is approached differently in different companies. Most companies work very hard to ensure and protect the anonymity of the people who provide feedback. In the case of organizations like Digital Equipment Corporation, however, where advanced, self-directed, team-based cultures are prevalent, recipients

of feedback know which individuals have provided specific comments and ratings; there is still a guideline that prevents any negative feedback from making it into an appraisal unless the rater has
previously given that feedback to the recipient.[4] This type of open
system, however, requires a high degree of maturity and mutual trust
on the part of all participants and is likely to succeed only in the
most advanced team-based organizations. We do not recommend it
to organizations using 360° feedback for the first time.

Assembling and Distributing Questionnaires

One of the most critical steps in administering any 360° written survey is the assembly of the questionnaire packets. Even organizations
using questionnaires that are completed electronically must attend
to this step.

Packets are typically made up of slightly different versions of the
questionnaire for each rater group (colleagues, direct reports, boss,
customers, and so forth), as well as answer sheets, return envelopes,
cover letters, and sets of instructions. When the packets have been
assembled, they are sent to the participant, who completes the self-
report and distributes the others to raters. (When raters have been
predetermined, questionnaires are usually sent to them directly.) A
deadline is stipulated for returning completed surveys for inclusion
in the participant's feedback.

Some organizations that purchase materials from outside vendors still prefer to handle packet assembly in-house to save on the
cost. To ensure the proper assembly and presentation of the packets, we recommend that a questionnaire administrator from the
vendor's firm spend time on-site to train the designated internal
people and go through a few practice rounds. This provides an opportunity to talk about what could go wrong and to solve any problems before they impede the process.

In our experience, the way the packets are collated can make or
break people's perceptions of the feedback process. Put yourself in a
participant's place. If you received a large envelope stuffed with

what seemed like incredible amounts of paper that you had to read and make sense of, you would probably not feel very enthusiastic about participating but would want to toss the entire package into the recycling bin instead. You might also feel that, if so little care was used in assembling the package, the promise of confidentiality would probably be treated in just as cavalier a fashion.

If, on the other hand, you received neatly collated sets of questionnaires, with your name printed on them and with clear, concise directions for completing and distributing them, you would have a more positive feeling about the process from the beginning.

Provide a Hotline

Even the clearest of directions will not guarantee that participants will take the time to read them; people are more likely than not to start reading the questions and filling out the answer sheets right away. Still, when they come across an item that confuses them, or if they have a question about how to complete or distribute the survey, you must provide them with a quick and easy way to get help. That is why we strongly recommend making it as easy as possible for participants by establishing a toll-free hotline for questions about completing the survey. The hotline phone number should be printed on the questionnaire.

Tips and Pointers

Here is a checklist you can use for administering the questionnaire packets that will help you avoid many of the problems associated with this phase of the 360° process:

- Print the questionnaires before distribution with as much information as possible (for example, participants' names).
- Print a return deadline on the questionnaires in large, noticeable letters; make the deadline a few days before the actual "drop-dead" date, to allow for late responses.

- Collate questionnaire materials into ready-to-send packets for each rater; this eliminates confusion and saves time for participants.
- Provide immediately visible, clear, concise directions with each questionnaire packet.
- Provide the toll-free hotline phone number in a prominent place on the questionnaire.
- Put important reminders in prominent lettering at the beginning and end of the questionnaire or response form (for example: *Please use a #2 lead pencil to complete this answer sheet*).
- Use a graphic to illustrate how and how not to fill in machine-readable bubble sheets.
- Consider including a #2 lead pencil with each rater's packet when using machine-readable answer sheets.

Processing the Questionnaires

The data from multiple-choice written questionnaires are the most straightforward to collect and process, because the response scales are standardized. Such scales also have the benefit of allowing computer generation of composite and normative data. Once the feedback has been collected, the data from the answer sheets are read by an optical scanner and entered into a computerized scoring program. The program then sorts and processes the data and prints out feedback reports for each individual, as well as group or composite reports, if applicable.

Potential Problems

This process, which can go extremely smoothly, depends almost entirely on the respondents' completing the answer sheets correctly. We do not live in a perfect world, however, so despite people's best efforts, there are often problems along the way.

Unknown Relationship to Recipient. Raters do not always re-member to fill out the section on the answer form where they indi-cate their work relationship to the recipient (for example, "This person is my boss," "This person reports to me," and so forth). One way of avoiding this problem is to instruct participants (preferably during a facilitated meeting) to fill in the appropriate relationship bubble for each of their selected raters before sending them the questionnaire packets to complete. Other options are to use differ-ent-colored answer sheets or answer sheets that have clear, printed labels for each respondent group. Participants must then be sure, however, to immediately put each packet in an envelope with the rater's name to avoid mix-ups.

Exchange of Answer Sheets. Sometimes, people inadvertently dis-tribute the answer sheets incorrectly. This can happen in several ways: a participant may accidentally give a rater his or her self-report to fill out, while filling out the rater questionnaire as a self-report; raters of different participants can decide to swap answer sheets (which have been pre-coded as belonging to those participants) in a mistaken attempt to ensure anonymity; or a rater might give his or her packet to someone else to fill out, who might have a different re-lationship to the participant.

More Questionnaires Returned Than Sent. Let us assume that, your conscientious attempts notwithstanding, you have received more completed questionnaires for a participant than were distrib-uted in the first place. First, look at all the person's answer sheets to see if any have been altered (as in the name-changing example above). If you have preprinted participants' names, this step will uncover the root of the problem. If answer sheets were not pre-printed, however, and you have more responses for a rater category than were distributed, your tracking sheet will come in handy.

Tracking sheets are used to record questionnaire distribution and response status for each rater group. This should be an auto-mated process. As answer sheets are scanned, the responses can be automatically updated, allowing the administrator to monitor the status of returns in real-time.

The tracking sheet will tell you how many questionnaires were distributed to and received from each rater group by participant, so if all responses have been received, you will notice any discrepancies. For example, you might see that you received four questionnaires from direct reports when only three were sent out, while only four have come back from colleagues when five were sent out. In this case, any number of things could have happened—the raters miscoded themselves, the recipient incorrectly recorded the number of questionnaires that were distributed, the recipient distributed additional questionnaires after mailing in the forms—to give some examples.

To resolve this dilemma, one option is to have the program administrator speak with the recipient to clarify how many questionnaires were actually distributed. Sometimes, a client will establish guidelines for what to do if there are too few raters for a respondent group. For example, you might be asked to combine raters from different groups (putting direct reports and colleagues in the same category) or to eliminate the respondent group entirely for that recipient. Sometimes, the questionnaire itself can provide clues on how to handle the situation. If it includes a section to be completed by direct reports only, for example, the vendor, with the client's permission, can make a judgment call about which rater group the answers should be applied to if the relationship has not been coded.

Written Marks on the Scannable Form. People sometimes write comments on their answer sheets, which can spell disaster when machine-readable forms are used, since any extraneous marks result in scanning errors and unprocessable data. While the guidelines in the section on administering questionnaire packets will help prevent this from happening, including a separate page for open-ended questions and additional input almost always does away with the problem. When respondents are provided with a separate page for additional comments, they feel no need to write them on the bubble sheet.

Late Returns. Perhaps the most common problems have to do with the time pressures caused by late responses. Late responses can take a variety of forms, from faxed-back answer sheets that cannot be optically scanned and therefore must be hand-entered into the computer, to already late responses sent by regular mail instead of overnight courier, to an avalanche of last-minute responses for a single participant who was late distributing the questionnaire packets to raters. As mentioned above, if large amounts of data are received after the deadline, it becomes difficult to have feedback ready in time for the workshop.

One way to avoid these delays when using third-party vendors is to designate a central, internal person who will collect everyone's completed questionnaires and send them in batches to the vendor for processing. (This approach will be described further.) Another is to provide postage-paid or business-reply return envelopes in which raters can immediately mail their completed questionnaires. Formally designating time within work hours to complete the feedback surveys, such as a group orientation meeting, can also help respondents avoid last-minute rushes, and in so doing give them the opportunity to be more thoughtful and reflective when answering the questions.

Certainly, the best way to deal with such problems is to prevent their occurrence in the first place. The questionnaire administrator must explain to the client contact at the outset (or to participants during an orientation session) what the ramifications are of each of these actions: less accurate feedback, less feedback in general, feedback that is not as useful. We have also found it very helpful for the administrator to detail for participants and the client contact, step by step, what happens to the completed questionnaires when they are returned for processing. Only when participants have a clear understanding of the whole process can they fully appreciate the necessity of complying with the instructions and guidelines.

Using Technology to Solve Administrative Problems

There are also certain technological approaches that can help you avoid some of these pitfalls. One increasingly popular method is to use computerized, or on-line, instruments. Here, participants and raters complete the survey electronically, either through a computer network, floppy disk, or CD-ROM, then e-mail or modem their responses back to the collecting party—and potentially even directly into the scoring program—for compilation and processing. This approach also allows participants to distribute questionnaires to raters more quickly (for example, over a network). With less paper involved and immediate access to and delivery of surveys, the process becomes less time-consuming and more efficient.

Before adopting this approach, however, you should ensure that all potential respondents are comfortable with the technology and have equal access to a network or computer and electronic delivery methods (e-mail or modems) for providing the feedback. The client and vendor must also be sure their hardware and software are compatible. Confidentiality and anonymity must be adequately safeguarded, too.

Advances are also being made in optical scanning technology that will result in competitively priced scanners that can read faxed forms. While this capability exists today in a few high-end machines, their cost is prohibitive for all but some professional feedback processing vendors—who must also decide if the purchase of such scanners is justified by the number of faxed responses they receive.

Self-scoring

Once the questionnaire feedback has been gathered, it can usually be either self-scored by the participant or scored by outside consultants (although some instruments are not hand-scorable). Self-scoring has the advantage of allowing the participant to receive the feedback immediately, and it is less expensive than using third-party scoring. But since completed forms are sent directly to recipients, and they may recognize the handwriting on the open-ended responses, raters are less anonymous, and their feedback may therefore be less honest. Furthermore, if the self-scored feedback is not presented or explained by an experienced facilitator, the data may confuse or even overwhelm the recipient.

Using Third Parties

To avoid the pitfalls outlined above, many organizations choose to send the questionnaires to outside consultants for processing. Having feedback data processed by a third party, which usually involves optical scanning and computerized generation of reports, also enables participants to receive the normative and composite data discussed previously.

If third-party scoring is the chosen route, questionnaires can either be collected by a central person within the organization (for instance, an administrator in the human resources or personnel department) and then sent all together to the outside firm to be scored, or sent directly by participants to the outside firm.

Although collecting the questionnaires in-house may make for greater company control and may lower certain direct costs, the administrative time and effort entailed should not be underestimated. In addition to ensuring timely completion and return of questionnaires by participants and raters, the internal resource must keep track of the response status for each participant: how many questionnaires were sent out and to whom, how many have been returned and by whom. The inside person must also maintain constant communication with the third-party representatives and consult with them whenever a problem or question arises. Finally, raters sometimes fear that the confidentiality of their responses will be compromised, since the internal person receiving their questionnaires could decide to read them.

Even when collection and administration are handled by third-party consultants, it is a good idea for the organization to designate an internal resource who will be responsible for ensuring that each rater is contacted (either by the participant or directly) and reminded to complete and return the questionnaire when the deadline approaches and a participant has an insufficient number of responses. It is equally important for the consultants involved to establish a good working relationship with this person so that any tracking or deadline problems can be resolved quickly.

Written Comments

If you are planning to include open-ended questions on the feedback instrument, you should be aware that they are more time-consuming to process, especially since raters' handwriting is sometimes difficult to decipher. Written comments can also compromise respondents' anonymity by making it easier for a recipient to identify who said what, based on what the comment is about or how it is worded. Finally, in cases where the open-ended data are combined with questionnaire data in a feedback report, some training and development professionals believe that recipients may tend to focus only on one or two written comments, while ignoring the message of the quantitative data.

Nevertheless, written comments do provide the recipient with much richer, more descriptive data than straight numerical ratings. Perhaps the optimal solution is to provide a combination of written and quantitative feedback, with the open-ended questions building and expanding on the multiple-choice items. In this way, recipients will be less likely to focus only on the verbal feedback, since it relates directly to the quantitative data and offers specific examples to which they can link their ratings. By choosing open-ended questions that build on certain key items, rather than having the whole questionnaire be open-ended, you can also cut down on processing time. We have found that this combination makes for a much more meaningful feedback experience for recipients.

Frequency of Feedback Gathering

How often should you gather feedback? In general, implementing the process with your target population about once a year will enable them to benchmark results and gauge their ongoing progress. If the feedback is being used as part of a professional development plan for individual managers, however, you may want to conduct the process in a time frame that is consistent with the managers' strategies for change. And naturally, if the feedback is being linked to performance reviews, the data collection should be scheduled so that results can be incorporated into the appraisals.

Concluding Remarks

A systematic, smoothly functioning administrative process frees up the feedback providers and recipients to concentrate on the content of the feedback, rather than getting bogged down in procedural details. It also reinforces their confidence in the feedback initiative, which means raters will be more candid, and recipients will be more inclined to take their assessments seriously. Thus, what may seem like merely mechanical aspects of the process can be key contributors to its success.

Chapter Seven

Holding Up the Mirror

Presenting the Feedback

A change of the heart is the essence of all other
change, and it is brought about by the re-education
of the mind.

—*Emmeline Pethick-Lawrence*

In Walt Disney's *Snow White and the Seven Dwarfs*, the wicked
queen self-confidently demands of her magic mirror, "Mirror, mirror on the wall, who's the fairest of them all?" When, to her horror,
the mirror brusquely reveals that her beauty has been surpassed by
Snow White's, the evil queen flies into a rage and plots her revenge.
In our opinion, the mirror's manner of presenting the feedback had
a great deal to do with the queen's reaction.

Imagine a similar situation: a manager who was reluctant to engage in the process in the first place asking her direct reports, peers,
and boss for feedback on her effectiveness as a leader. If the group's
reply is poorly timed, focuses only on negative behaviors, or is difficult to understand, the purpose of the effort will be lost. Worse yet,
the manager may react in the same way the queen did—by getting
angry and harming those who are responsible for the feedback.

While 360° feedback is a powerful tool—a mirror that reveals a
manager's effectiveness from the various points of view of those he
or she works with closely—like the truth-telling magic mirror, it
may give us information we did not expect and do not want to hear.
That is why decisions concerning the forum for presenting and interpreting the feedback can be as important as choosing the method
of data collection or the instrument.

While you may be gathering data on the right behaviors and ensuring that they are reliable, if the feedback is presented poorly and recipients are not able to make sense of it and use it to plan their development, the entire process will have been a waste of everyone's time. As a result, people may harbor ill feelings toward those who initiated the process and those who provided the feedback. And beyond that, they will learn nothing about themselves and how to improve their effectiveness within the organization.

In this chapter, we will take a look at what you need to do to help recipients get the most out of the feedback process. We will review the barriers that keep people from accepting their feedback, your options for how to present the feedback, and a typical work session agenda.

Ensuring That People Get the Most Out of the 360° Feedback Experience

In Chapter Five, we discussed how to negotiate the obstacles that could make people reluctant to embark on the 360° process. Having addressed those issues, you will also need to eliminate the factors that can prevent people from getting the most out of the experience. Here, we will focus on two key elements of the presentation: the work session in which recipients first receive their feedback and the report on each manager's data. Again, we will provide ideas on how you can create enthusiasm for the process and increase the likelihood that the feedback will be used to achieve individual and organizational goals.

Why People Reject Feedback

As one of our associates, Harold Scharlatt, puts it, "No one is indifferent to feedback."[1] At times, it is this very lack of indifference—people's sense that whatever they are going to hear about themselves is important—that creates problems. Says John Hoffman, a facilitator who has had extensive experience presenting feedback, "Managers are afraid of getting news they don't want and won't like."[2]

In many cases, participants' first reaction may be to look for ways to rationalize the information to better fit their self-perceptions or idealized views of themselves. Our experience suggests that an unwillingness or inability to challenge self-perceptions is one of the three most common reasons that people reject their feedback. The other two are a fear of having weaknesses exposed and the perception that the feedback is unbalanced. Understanding and addressing these potential barriers will enable you to design a successful work session. While you cannot control how people feel coming into the session, you can certainly relieve their anxiety once they are there by maintaining their self-esteem and providing a constructive experience.

Unwillingness to Challenge Self-perceptions. Most people who have experienced a degree of success in their careers will attribute that success to, among other things, their own capability and expertise. A strong belief in oneself and one's ability is frequently a characteristic of successful people in organizations. Their current styles and behaviors are what got them to where they are today. So why mess with a sure thing? Challenging this self-perception is difficult and usually not high on people's agendas.

This obstacle becomes less of an issue when people see feedback as a contributing factor to continuous learning and improvement. As one technology manager in a large pharmaceuticals company remarked, "It never feels good to find out that the people you work with believe that you're more focused on your agenda than theirs or that you're not spending enough time with your team. But the way I see it, the more I know about how others see me and what they expect from me, the more effective I can be. It's ammunition to improve my performance."

Robert Kaplan, in *Beyond Ambition*,[3] describes four phases of self-development—maintaining the old self, separating from the old self, exploring the new self, and reinforcing the new self. As Kaplan explains, "The first phase is a pre-change phase in which the manager puts most of his or her energy into maintaining the existing self. The individual may receive cues that suggest a need for change, but these are generally deflected. Whatever adjustments the individual might

make in this phase are kept comfortably within the existing system—that is, the existing 'self-system.' "[4]

If you believe that Kaplan's first phase is the context for the initial presentation of feedback, how do you ensure that people will be
open to hearing information that contradicts their sense of themselves? When their belief in their abilities is challenged, the validity of the data is often challenged as well. Positioning the feedback
as a single snapshot of the individual at a specific point in time will
better enable people to accept the messages others are sending
them. Emphasizing that this is not the absolute and final truth
about the recipient will help put the feedback into perspective.

Changing a person's self-image is a slow and difficult process.
During the initial review of the feedback, we ask only that people
walk away with one or two key learnings, not that they get every
message from which they might benefit. When people are allowed
to hold on to what they see as the fundamental elements of their
success, they are more accepting of information that challenges
their image of themselves. It is our belief that, given the proper
guidance and support, additional insights will come over time.

During a recent feedback session, a senior investment banker became quite vocal about his reactions to data he perceived as negative and attempted to disprove each data point one by one, arguing
that people just did not understand the requirements of his job and
the pressure he was under. Instead of trying to defend the feedback
he had received, we listened in silence and then began to ask questions about what was going on in the organization that might cause
people to misperceive him. He seemed surprised that we were not
trying to convince him; gradually, his tone and attitude changed,
and he seemed more comfortable with the idea that some of the data
might be relevant. He even acknowledged that there could be reasons for people responding the way they did.

In situations like this, it is generally better to let recipients argue
with and reject some of their feedback, even if the data seem perfectly plausible. By letting recipients vent, you are clearing the way
for them to acknowledge and accept at least a few of the messages

they received and thereby increasing the likelihood that they will act on them.

Fear of Exposing Weaknesses. No one wants to look ineffectual or foolish—particularly managers, who are conscious of the need to appear confident and self-assured to those around them. By asking people to rate our behavior, however, we run the risk of having our weaknesses exposed—weaknesses we either compensate for or keep hidden and have never shared with anyone.

To minimize the anxiety associated with having one's weaknesses brought out into the open, make sure that people are given complete control of their feedback during the session. They should be allowed to make choices about what results they will share, and how. They should never be required to show or discuss their specific feedback with others. Any group activity should be focused on the participants' analyses and conclusions from the data, not on their specific results for any scales or items. This type of control enables people to concentrate on understanding the data rather than protecting their self-esteem. In addition, if they do elect to share what they have learned after the session, they should be given guidance on how to do so effectively. In our experience, focusing on learning and next steps, as opposed to specific numbers and ratings, is the most effective approach.

Unbalanced Feedback. Another factor that influences the acceptance of feedback is the message itself. Obviously, positive feedback is more readily accepted than negative feedback, since it tends to fit with our own self-image. Feedback should give people a sense of what behaviors they ought to continue, not just what they ought to do differently. Such an emphasis not only provides a more accurate, balanced picture of the person's overall effectiveness, it also increases the probability that having examined the good news, the recipient will be open to hearing the bad as well.

What does this mean for how the feedback should be presented? It means that the facilitators, through the design of the work session, must ensure that there will be as strong a focus on strengths as on weaknesses during the analysis and consolidation of the feedback. People should have an opportunity to identify—and celebrate—those behaviors and characteristics that have served them well and contributed to their success. Before they start considering how to overcome or compensate for their weaknesses, they should decide how they will leverage their strengths. John Hoffman observes, "In almost every workshop, there is someone who gets all good ratings except from one rater or in one area—and the less positive feedback tends to negate the positive data in the person's mind. As a facilitator, part of my job is to bring people back to a consideration of their strengths."[5]

Scheduling the Feedback Session

Once a manager has agreed to participate in the 360° effort, the feedback session should be scheduled as soon as possible. If there is a gap between when the questionnaires or interviews are completed and when participants get their results, people may begin to lose interest. In addition, if the organization is going through a restructuring or major change, people may no longer perceive the feedback as relevant.

Choosing the Location of the Feedback Session

As valuable and rich as the feedback may be, if people are unable to concentrate on the goals of the feedback session or remain focused on the behaviors they need to develop, it may not produce the desired results. We recommend selecting a location for review and analysis of the feedback that will ensure a minimum of interruptions, enable people to focus and concentrate on the task, and provide privacy if desired.

The Center for Creative Leadership offers several programs of varying duration that allow people the opportunity to focus on their development. While these programs may not be affordable for everybody, the idea of separating the feedback recipients from their daily grind can be applied to any workshop by holding the session in another building, such as a nearby hotel or conference center, or a conference room in another area of the building could be used. This helps eliminate interruptions, removes managers from other distractions, and lets recipients know that the event they are taking part in is seen as important.

Several organizations we have worked with have committed the resources to provide their own dedicated learning centers. Companies like The Coca-Cola Company, Household International, and General Electric have professionally run facilities that remove people from the day-to-day demands of their jobs and provide an environment in which they can focus only on themselves and their personal development.

Methods for Delivering the Feedback

There are three primary methods for getting the results of the feedback to participants—one-on-one meetings, group presentations, and self-study, which can be conducted using workbooks, diskettes, or CD-ROM. Your choice will depend on the level of the population you are working with, the nature of the feedback, and factors such as your budget, the availability of staff, the time frame for project completion, the location and availability of participants, and the extent to which feedback is valued and accepted in the organization.

No one forum for presenting the feedback is perfect. We will discuss the advantages and disadvantages of each approach from three points of view: the participant's perspective, delivery considerations, and the resources available.

One-on-one Feedback Delivery

For senior-level or high-potential managers, the one-on-one delivery session in which the recipient meets individually with the facilitator or coach to review and analyze the data is commonly chosen.

Says Penny Nieroth, "Higher-level people don't want to be part of a workshop. They want a more tailored program, and they often have tough issues to deal with that can't be discussed in a group."[6] Laura Daley-Caravella, an experienced feedback presenter, agrees. "Because it's so much more specific and in-depth, one-on-one feedback is more appropriate for senior executives, especially when someone is in trouble and needs a coach."[7]

Participant's Perspective. In group sessions, a recipient may have to compete for air time or engage in discussions on issues of no particular relevance to him or her. A one-on-one presentation, on the other hand, can be personalized to focus on the specific needs and interests of a single recipient. We recommend that a one-on-one session begin with a review of the recipient's key challenges and achievements during the past four to six months to see how they might have affected the feedback. The coach or facilitator can then help the recipient interpret the feedback within the context of his or her work environment, personality type, and decision-making style.

Confidentiality is another advantage. With no one else in the feedback session, the recipient can feel secure that the results will not become generally known. Organizations frequently prefer to have an outside consultant conduct the one-on-one feedback session to ensure an even greater level of confidentiality. In addition, the outsider presents an opportunity for "true confessions"—admissions of weaknesses or discussions of problems that the manager might not want to reveal to an inside person. Finally, a one-on-one meeting provides a context for recipients to talk about specific behavior changes required back on the job and to brainstorm about realistic next steps.

In a recent session conducted with a senior executive responsible for running several diverse businesses in three countries, the executive determined that priority setting was a key area for development. After a lengthy conversation about how, exactly, he needed to improve and what got in the way of his effectiveness, he admitted that in fact he knew how to set priorities but somehow rarely took the time to do it. Instead, he allowed himself to focus on the businesses he was best at and considered most enjoyable. Only then did he identify his real need: managing his calendar to establish plans for all the businesses and allocate his own and others' time to each. The session ended with the executive pulling out his electronic calendar and plugging in blocks of time over a three-month period to do what for him was priority setting; in fact, what he was doing was establishing a discipline and a method for planning how to manage each business. It is unlikely that this kind of solution would have resulted from a group session.

Delivery Considerations.   Since most people's behavior patterns are well entrenched, especially if they have led to success, hearing the messages of change that the feedback may suggest and determining what to do about them can require the special attention of a coach. The person presenting the feedback can act as a sounding board and confidant to help get the recipient through what could be an arduous process of self-examination and soul searching.

Because the coaching role is so important, having the right chemistry between the facilitator and the feedback recipient is crucial to success. The facilitator of a one-on-one feedback session must be able to gain the recipient's trust and help him or her use the feedback to bring about meaningful change. In particular, the facilitator must have a sure sense of when to confront a recipient with painful truths and when to back off.

Resource Considerations.   One-on-one sessions are easy to schedule, since there is only one participant's time to consider. Given the demanding work schedules most people must deal with, this is an important consideration.

On the other hand, meeting with people one-on-one requires a lot of time, especially when you are dealing with a large number of recipients. If you assume that each session will last about two to three hours, it is difficult to meet with more than two people a day.

In addition, more than one meeting may be necessary to help the person internalize the data and develop next steps.

Group Feedback Workshops

Many organizations bring fifteen to twenty people together for a one- or two-day workshop. A description of a typical workshop can be found later in this chapter.

Participant's Perspective.   A group workshop provides a supportive environment and serves to reassure people that they are not the only ones getting negative feedback. Some managers actually become more receptive to their feedback when they see that people they respect respond to feedback in a positive manner.

When someone is particularly affected or surprised by negative messages, a group can often help that person think through those messages, understand the reasons for the feedback, and put it into proper perspective. They can also make suggestions for development. Receiving negative feedback is a highly emotional experience for many people, and it helps boost overall team morale to experience it together. As Nieroth says, "The workshop setting allows them to support each other, as well as to explore and validate the messages that came through the feedback."[8] Daley-Caravella observes, "It can be important for people to realize that they are not alone; they are not the only ones experiencing this. Also, they often have an opportunity to see someone they really respect get less-than-perfect feedback—it makes them realize that everyone has weaknesses."[9]

Despite the benefits to be derived from the support and insight of group members, however, some people will feel uneasy at the thought that others will know about their weaknesses. Although an individual's feedback should never be distributed for group consumption, people may still feel uncomfortable asking questions aloud that could give clues to the messages they received. Thus, a lack of privacy may mean participants will not get their feedback clarified as much as they need to. To some degree, the problem can be solved by holding small-group sessions in which individuals can spread out and work with others or privately.

Delivery Considerations. One advantage of group workshops is that they provide an opportunity to practice the skills being evaluated. People get a chance to use these skills in a controlled setting and to receive additional feedback on their effectiveness before applying them back on the job. This often gives them more confidence both in the data and in themselves and increases the likelihood that they will change their behavior.

Another advantage of this method of delivery is that most feedback workshops designed to support a purchased questionnaire are easily adapted to fit into an organization's training curriculum. A feedback workshop can take from three hours to two days to deliver and can be integrated into a longer training session encompassing other development goals of the organization or team.

While a conscientious facilitator will always try to work with each person individually at some time during the session, time constraints and the number of people at the program limit the amount of individual attention any one person can receive. People may not get the most out of their feedback without someone asking the right questions to help them draw the right conclusions. If you anticipate that a group of people will have a difficult time digesting their feedback, consider extending the session to allow time for personal attention, or invite people to sign up for one-on-one sessions during breaks, at lunch, or in the evening.

Resource Considerations. Scheduling a one- or two-day workshop for a group of fifteen to twenty busy people can be difficult. A way to work around potential scheduling conflicts is to break the workshop into modules. In the first module, present the feedback and have each person identify behaviors in need of development. Then, schedule skills-training workshops that address specific development needs. Managers can fit the appropriate workshops into their schedules.

Offsetting the scheduling problems inherent in the group delivery method is its cost-effectiveness. Obviously, working with up to twenty people simultaneously is much less costly than holding twenty one-on-one sessions, especially if the organization is using outside facilitators.

Self-study

As the name implies, the self-study approach calls for people to get their feedback reports, review and analyze the data, and identify next steps on their own, with the help of a self-paced guide that can take the form of either a printed workbook or an electronic program. The interactive nature of CD-ROM technology makes the process of reviewing and analyzing the feedback report akin to working with a facilitator. We believe, however, that although CD-ROM technology has tremendous promise, at the time of this writing it cannot yet provide the kind of assistance and guidance to be obtained from working with a trained facilitator.

Participant's Perspective.   Self-study guides that accompany or are part of a feedback report are useful when people do not want to take more time out of their busy schedules than necessary. The recipient can take the report and the guide home or to a quiet place to review the feedback at his or her convenience. These guides, whether booklets or electronic programs, work best with people who have had prior experience with receiving and analyzing 360° feedback.

Nevertheless, most organizations prefer not to rely on self-study guides, which can only ask a set of predetermined questions to aid in the interpretation of the data. These questions are rarely specific enough to get people thinking about the work context in which the feedback was given or the subtleties and implications of the feedback. Nor can a computer program or a feedback report alone help people work through the emotions they are likely to feel when they receive their feedback.

Delivery Considerations. The unstructured nature of the self-study method requires managers to be responsible for finding the time to review the feedback. Although some managers appreciate the flexibility, others find that the pressure of other, higher-priority activities leads to long delays. Some never get to the task until so much time has passed that the data's usefulness is eroded. In addition, left to their own devices, people may not take the feedback as far as it can go in helping them overcome behavioral weaknesses. Development plans may be incomplete or weak when no one else is there to offer suggestions, ask questions, and serve as a sounding board. Additionally, recipients get no chance to practice the skills that are the focus of their development plans.

This delivery method also carries with it a risk that the feedback will be misinterpreted. All the personal issues and questions that can turn into barriers to acceptance cannot be anticipated or addressed in even the most user-friendly feedback report or interactive computer program. For that reason, it is vital that the report or guidebook be especially clear and easy to understand, although even then there is a danger that, with no one available to answer questions about interpreting the data, they may be ignored or misused.

Resource Considerations. One obvious advantage of the self-study delivery method is its low cost. Eliminating facilitators and the need to bring a group of people together for a day or more greatly reduces the expense of delivering the feedback.

Choosing the Right Approach for Your Organization

As you narrow your options for the delivery of the feedback, keep in mind the following questions:

- What form does the feedback take?
- How many people will be receiving feedback?

- What is the time frame for getting the feedback to the recipients? How difficult will it be to deliver all the feedback within your time frame?
- What staff resources and budget can you dedicate to the project?
- How familiar are recipients with 360° feedback?

Your answers to these questions, along with the information about the delivery options summarized in the chart shown in Exhibit 7.1, should enable you to select the method that will work best for you, the recipients, and your organization.

Making Sure Your Chosen
Feedback Delivery Method Is Effective

Earlier in this chapter, we identified three reasons that people resist feedback, and we suggested ways to overcome that resistance: by giving people control over their data, by making sure they do not lose sight of their positive feedback and concentrate wholly on the negative, and by seeing to it that they understand the extent to which the data explain and account for their overall effectiveness. Whatever delivery method you use to present the feedback to recipients and ensure that they get the key messages from the data, there are four requirements for making the experience successful.

Explain the Underlying Model Being Used

The questions you have asked about people's behavior should be based on a model that describes the behaviors that are important for effectiveness on the job and why they are effective.[10] Whenever possible, this model should be explained to people so they can relate their feedback and the need to modify their behavior to their specific situation, objectives, and priorities. The technical report should be made available to people who are interested in learning

Exhibit 7.1. A Comparison of Feedback Delivery Options

Method	Participant's Perspective	Delivery Considerations	Resource Considerations
One-on-one	Personalized Highly confidential	One-on-one coaching available Skilled facilitator required	Easy to schedule Time-intensive Costly
Group workshop	Supportive environment Less privacy	Opportunity for skill practice Less individual attention	Potential scheduling conflicts Cost-effective
Self-study	Convenient No interaction	Requires self-motivation Carries possibility that data may be misinterpreted Works best when recipient is 360° savvy	Low per-person cost Easy to schedule

more about how the model was developed and what research went into formulating the questions. One caution—a model that is too complex may be worse than no model at all if it confuses people rather than helps them interpret the feedback.

Involve People in Interpreting the Data

In some systems, computer programs provide a narrative interpretation of the feedback and tell people what they must do to improve. Although this might sound like a very efficient approach, people who are responsible for making decisions about millions of dollars of company assets are likely to resent having a computer tell them to change their behavior. Given some assistance, most people are quite capable of evaluating their own feedback and determining its implications; they also know better than anyone else about special circumstances that have affected their results. Moreover, allowing people to interpret their feedback increases the likelihood that they will accept it and do something with it.

In fact, a computerized approach sometimes creates more problems than it solves. We once worked with a manager who had received a report saying she should do more clarifying. Her response was, "My team consists of seasoned professionals with an average of fifteen years experience. The work environment is stable, and the project parameters are clear and well understood. More clarifying on my part would be perceived as a sign that I don't trust them or am an inveterate micro-manager." As it turned out, the report was based on a scoring program that told the computer to find items that were rated as very important but that received a low frequency rating and to compile them in a list of developmental needs. It could not take into account the specific environmental and situational factors at work. And the perception that the assessment was inaccurate caused the manager to regard the rest of her report with suspicion.

Have Each Person Develop an Improvement Plan

Feedback is more likely to result in behavior change if the manager develops an improvement plan with specific targets and realistic strategies for achieving them. Such action planning encourages people to take control of their lives and to decide for themselves how to become more effective. Moreover, in combination with a theory to guide the process, the action planning will help people learn how to analyze the specific needs of their situation.

Choose a Credible Facilitator to Manage the Process

Whether you are using a group method or delivering the feedback one-on-one, the capability of the person selected to run the session is critical. That person sets the tone, serves as the primary resource to help people understand their feedback, and assists them in devising strategies for overcoming any obstacles to meeting their development targets. We will discuss the facilitator's role in more detail later in this chapter.

The Group Work Session

Because it allows them to engage many people in the process quickly and cost-effectively, decision makers often opt for the group workshop method of delivering feedback. Next, we describe two approaches we have found to be practical and engaging. The first is to conduct a workshop that focuses on creating an awareness of how others perceive the feedback recipient. The second is to conduct another type of workshop, one that builds on this awareness and provides skill-development activities to help people apply new behaviors back on the job. Additional examples of feedback displays and workshop designs are presented in the Resource A section at the end of the book.

Approach I—Creating Awareness

The first type of workshop includes three components: presenting the feedback, coaching group activities, and preparing for a sharing and clarifying meeting.

Presenting the Feedback

This segment of the workshop begins with a brief overview of the research and model upon which the questionnaire is based. Participants learn that they will receive information on how important each practice is to the effective performance of their jobs (as reported by their bosses), how frequently they currently use each practice (as reported by direct reports, colleagues, and their bosses), and how frequently people would like them to use the practice.

Before participants get their individual feedback reports, they are given a few key pointers for getting the most out of their feedback. These include:

Pay attention to your first impression of the data.

We typically have an immediate reaction to the data we see. They either make us feel great (Hey, I didn't know I was doing that!) or terrible (I can't believe people see me that way!). There is no real reason to fight the feeling, but we do need to move through it in order to see the data for what they represent.

Focus on the messages, not just the measures.

Recipients must look at the data in the context of their jobs— the nature of their work, the goals they are trying to achieve, and the skill and experience of their team members. High ratings are not always good, and low ratings are not always bad. For example, low frequency ratings in Monitoring may not be bad news for some-one working with an experienced team in a reasonably stable envi-ronment. However, high frequency ratings in the same situation may raise concerns of micro-managing or lack of confidence in oth-ers' ability. Also, to go beyond the averages or the numbers per se, recipients should look at the relative highs and lows, as well as pat-terns that might appear either within or between the scales.

Appreciate the perceptions of others.

Recipients may believe that other people's perceptions of them are incorrect—that their raters neither understand their jobs nor understand the demands and constraints they must work with— and they may even be right. Unfortunately, in this case, being right is not worth much. Ratings reflect the manager's effect on others, not his or her intent. The questions recipients need to ask them-selves, therefore, are, "What am I doing that causes people to see me differently than I see myself?" or "What is going on in the orga-nization that could affect people's perceptions of me?"

Importance Feedback. The feedback is presented in blocks of information, which allows people time to process and assimilate the data.[11] The first block of data is the importance feedback (see Exhibits

7.2 and 7.3). Ideally, a report should provide two views of this information: how the recipient and the boss rated each practice on a scale of 1 (not important) to 5 (absolutely essential), and the four practices the recipient and the boss identified as most essential practices for effectiveness on the job.

As people review this part of the report, we ask them to consider the following questions to guide them in their analysis and interpretation:

- Which practices do you and your boss agree are the most important to the effective performance of your job? On which practices do you disagree?
- What issues need to be clarified or discussed with your boss?
- Based on this information, which practices would you say are most critical for the effective performance of your job?

Feedback on Frequency of Use. When recipients analyze the data on how frequently raters perceive that they are using specific practices and behaviors, they also have an opportunity to compare their own self-ratings with the ratings of their evaluators. The report (see Exhibit 7.4) should display the data using average scores, frequency distributions, and comparisons to national or industry norms (percentile scores).[12]

People are then asked to review this information, using the following questions as guides:

- Whom did you ask to provide you with feedback? Are they in a position to observe and evaluate your performance? To what extent do you depend on them to get work done? How important are these relationships?
- How consistent are the responses across rater groups (boss, colleagues, direct reports)? How consistent are the responses within each rater group?
- How consistent should they be? Are you trying to treat each rater the same, or have you been working with each rater differently based on their needs and the situation?

Exhibit 7.2. Importance Ratings

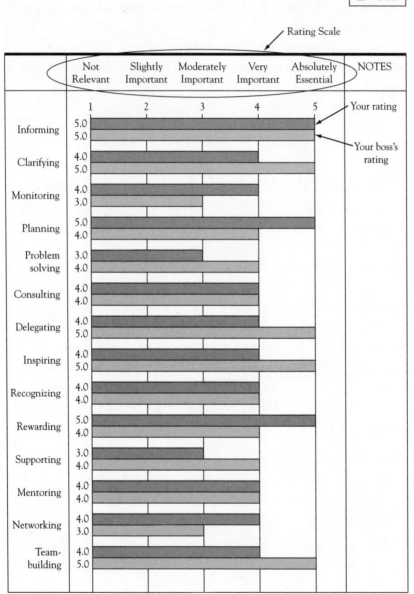

Exhibit 7.3. Importance Ratings—Most Important Practices

You completed a section of the Compass questionnaire that asked you to rate how important each managerial practice is to the effective performance of your job. Likewise, your boss rated the importance of each practice for your job.

Our research shows that all of these practices are frequently considered important or essential. However, some practices may be more important than others, based on the demands of your particular job. Therefore, both you and your boss selected the top four practices that are *most* important for your job.

Below, you'll find a display of top four practices selected by you and your boss. Look for similarities and differences between your view and your boss's view. If you and your boss have different opinions about which practices are most important for your job, you may want to schedule a meeting to come to a better understanding. It may be useful to discuss what each of you considers most important, and why.

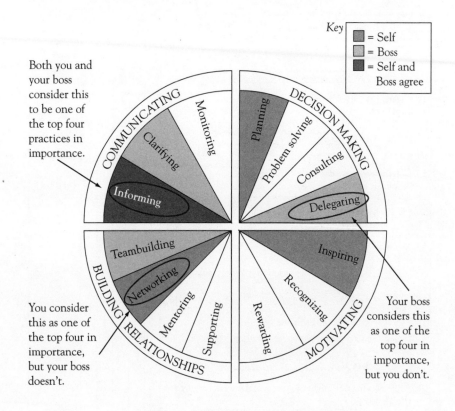

Exhibit 7.4. Scale Scores and Frequency Distribution

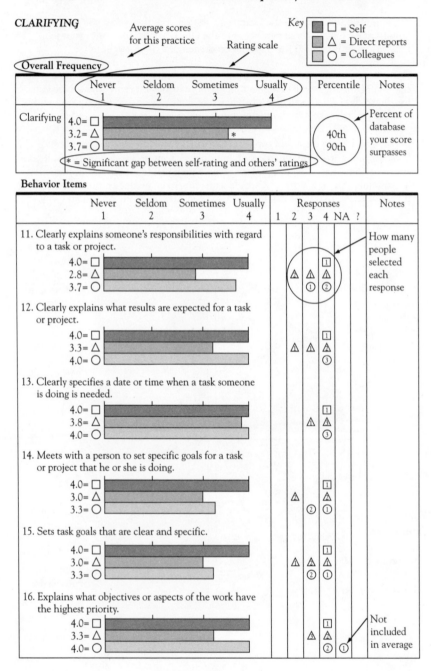

- What patterns emerge within each scale? Are there any patterns across the scales?
- To what extent do you agree with the opinions of those who completed the questionnaire on you?
- How do you compare with the database?

Recommendations. The third kind of information that should be provided consists of recommendations: how frequently people feel the recipient should use each practice in order to be most effective (Exhibit 7.5).[13] Here, managers have the opportunity to learn how many of their raters want them to use a particular practice less, more, or as often as they currently do. Coupled with the information on the importance and the frequency of use of the practice, this helps them zero in on strengths and weaknesses.

The following questions are provided as guidelines for interpretation:

- What are your strengths (high frequency of use, top quartile compared to database, the majority of raters recommending using the practice as much as you now do)?
- What areas need further development (low frequency of use, bottom quartile compared to database, the majority of raters recommending using it more or less)?
- How does this feedback fit with feedback you've received before? What surprises did you get? What was confirmed?
- What have people recommended you do more, the same, and less to improve your effectiveness?

Coaching Group Activities

After recipients have taken an initial pass at analyzing their feedback, the coaching group exercise provides an opportunity to discuss specific skills with other workshop participants. In our experience, the

Exhibit 7.5. Recommendations

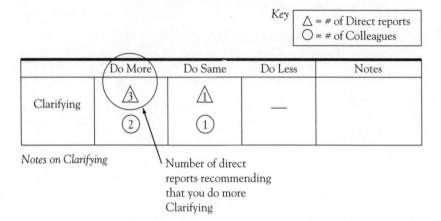

Key
△ = # of Direct reports	
○ = # of Colleagues	

	Do More	Do Same	Do Less	Notes
Clarifying	△3 ○2	△1 ○1	—	

Notes on Clarifying   Number of direct reports recommending that you do more Clarifying

most effective format is one that includes a structured, small-group discussion and a development guide for each practice—an easy-to-read supplementary set of materials that includes additional information about the practice, suggestions for when to use it more or less, and tips and pointers for using it more effectively on the job.

Preparing for a Sharing and Clarifying Meeting

The last component of the workshop we designed provides people with tools and techniques for finalizing development targets. These segments, although begun during the workshop, provide the foundation on which to build follow-up activities that help clarify feedback messages and ensure meaningful action back on the job. During the consolidation process, people are asked to isolate key strengths, weaknesses, and areas that need clarification.

As noted before, it is crucial to focus on strengths as well as weaknesses during this activity. The consolidated data become the basis for the sharing and clarifying meeting. We recommend that, before development targets are finalized, recipients meet with their raters to confirm their findings, clarify messages that were confusing, and get suggestions for actions that would improve effectiveness. Pointers on holding effective meetings with raters should be offered during the workshop. (Advice on consolidating data and on meeting with feedback providers is offered in the next chapter.)

Approach II—Creating Awareness and Skill Development

The most effective approach to skill development will first ensure that people understand the fundamentals of using each skill appropriately and then let them practice using the skills in situations that gradually get closer to what they might encounter in their jobs. Therefore, because this workshop provides skill practice in addition to creating awareness, it has several additional features.

Identifying a Business Challenge

To make the feedback even more relevant, as part of the pre-program preparation we ask people to identify a business challenge that currently confronts them and the people whose commitment they need to resolve the issue. Participants are then asked to distribute feedback questionnaires to the individuals they have identified as critical to their success in the situations they have identified. This provides two benefits—the feedback will be in the context of a real event and not generalized across many situations, and it is provided by the specific people they are currently trying to influence. Thus, the messages they receive are firmly anchored in the real world, which makes the learning more immediately useful.

Using Video Models

Video models are used to illustrate the effective use of the behaviors covered during the workshop. People can not only read about a given skill but also see examples of its effective use in various situations before they are asked to try using it themselves. Video models also ensure that the skills are presented in a consistent manner from group to group rather than relying solely on the capability of the instructor to demonstrate them clearly and effectively.

Using Case Studies

Once people understand the rudiments of the skill and have practiced using it in generic exercises, we give them the opportunity to practice it in a situation closer to home. As part of the pre-program preparation, we frequently develop case studies that describe typical situations people in the workshop face day-to-day. Such case studies involve role plays that begin the process of transferring what participants have learned back to their jobs. They are also the springboard for discussion of the unique aspects of the recipients' company and what it will take to use the skills effectively in their particular culture and organizational structure.

Rehearsing Skills

Finally, participants rehearse the skills in the context of a real job situation. We ask participants to use the business challenge they identified as part of the pre-program preparation or to select another situation in which they are currently involved. Using the other participants as resources and coaches, and following a plan they have devised with the help of guidelines provided by the facilitator, they rehearse what they would do and say in this situation. The rehearsal enables people to get additional feedback on their use of the skills and enhances their confidence in their ability to use them effectively in a real situation.

Choosing Facilitators and Coaches

People new to receiving 360° feedback often have a number of questions such as, "Why are these behaviors being measured?" "How can I use this information to enhance my performance?" "What next steps should I take?" The role of the facilitator is to help participants interpret their feedback and to answer any questions they have. If a facilitator is unable or unwilling to provide the answers to important questions, participants may become skeptical about both their own feedback and the feedback process in general.

For that reason, facilitators must be able to talk intelligently about the model on which the behavior items are based, the development of the instrument and its correlation to effectiveness on the job, and the specific behavior items and how they relate to each other. They must be able to help recipients put the feedback into context, identify key themes and patterns of behavior, clarify next steps to address weaknesses and leverage strengths, and answer the various questions people ask.

It is essential for facilitators to have gone through a 360° feedback experience themselves. They will then be much better able to put themselves in the place of the participants, feel the same feelings, and understand the importance of their role in analyzing the data.

Internal or External Facilitators?

You have two options when you are deciding who should facilitate the group workshop or present individual feedback—you can use internal or external facilitators.

Depending on the size of your organization, the number of managers participating in the feedback program, and the expertise available within the human resource department, an internal facilitator may be the best choice to deliver the workshop or present individual feedback. The advantages to using an internal facilitator include familiarity with the organization's development objectives and the culture and environment in which its managers operate. To present the feedback effectively, facilitators need to understand how the feedback program relates to other organizational efforts and goals.

An inventory of your available internal resources may reveal a need to look outside the organization for a facilitator. If you are using an outside vendor to develop, administer, collect, and process the feedback, you may want to use a facilitator from the same firm to ensure familiarity with the instrument or process. To be effective, however, an external resource must also understand the issues the feedback process is trying to address, the internal dynamics of your company and its culture, and the people with whom he or she will be working. In many cases, such understanding can be gained by briefing external facilitators on the overall development goals of the organization or allowing them to meet or speak with a cross-section of the managers who will receive feedback before the program is launched.

Managers receiving feedback often appreciate having a third party involved. An outside person can both help recipients get a feel for what people in other companies are doing and increase the sense of confidentiality among the recipients.

Facilitator Certification

If an organization prefers to use internal trainers, a train-the-trainer program is often the answer. Most vendors offer a two- or three-day program to train in-house resources in the use of their instrument. Usually, a certified trainer experienced in delivering 360° feedback begins by facilitating a program with the would-be trainers as participants to give them a sense of what it is like to look in the mirror and get feedback on their own behaviors. The consultant then answers questions about the process and the instrument. Finally, the potential trainers get to practice presenting key information and analyzing sample reports, with the consultant providing coaching and offering suggestions for improvement.

The certification process generally includes having the consultants observe the newly trained facilitators when they deliver their first programs. Frequently, the vendor will also provide follow-up and coaching as needed to ensure that the programs are running smoothly. They may also review program evaluations as a source of tips and ideas for improved performance.

Skill Level and Experience

A skilled facilitator can add a lot of value to the feedback, while an untrained or clumsy facilitator can render it virtually useless. To make the most of the feedback experience for participants, facilitators need to be skilled at spotting trends in the data, pulling out key messages, and helping participants interpret their feedback. A facilitator should also have experience in a classroom setting, effective speaking and listening skills, and the knowledge and experience to cite real-life examples of people using effective managerial and leadership behaviors. A well-designed feedback report will help managers work through the meaning of individual items and scores, but a gifted facilitator can move them from understanding to action.

Concluding Remarks

However you choose to present the feedback in your organization, everyone involved should be conscious of its potential impact. After all, these are not data about production quotas or budget parameters but evaluations of people's individual styles, skills, and effectiveness. Because of people's sensitivity to this type of feedback, the process should always be designed to maximize their willingness to act on the information they receive. Presenters should be prepared to respond not only to what recipients say but also to less explicit emotional reactions. By helping feedback recipients to understand and work through their reactions during the presentation process, they can clear the way for the next stage: translating the feedback into action back on the job.

Chapter Eight

Creating Lasting Change

Follow-up Activities

It is of no profit to have learned well, if you do not
do well.

—Publilius Syrus

Once people have had a chance to analyze and interpret their feedback, they must decide where they are going to devote their energies, that is, what changes in their behavior they are going to work on achieving and what development strategies will be most effective at bringing about those changes.

At this point in the process, people may be seeing themselves in ways they never have before. Whatever their new image of themselves, they must now use the insight they have gained to plan for their own development. In our experience, this is a critical juncture in the 360° process. If participants do not take meaningful steps to translate their feedback into action within two weeks of leaving the work session, they will probably never do so.

In this chapter, we will examine follow-up activities that occur after the data have been analyzed and interpreted. Some of these activities begin during the work session and are completed by recipients when they return to their jobs. These include consolidating the feedback, identifying strengths and preliminary development targets, and holding meetings with raters to share results and clarify next steps. Other follow-up activities are the primary responsibility of the individual, with the support of the manager and coach. Such activities include final identification of strengths and development targets, deciding on strategies for change, preparing and using a development plan, and linking the feedback to formal human re-source systems within the organization.

Consolidating the Feedback

Most 360° feedback reports are data-rich, providing so much infor-mation that they often raise more questions than they answer. Be-fore people can establish development targets and plans, therefore, they need to confirm their findings and finalize their assessments. As a means of consolidating their data, the first thing people need to do is make sense of the information they have and identify what they still need to find out. While there are many possible formats for ac-complishing this, the one we have found most helpful is shown in Exhibit 8.1.[1]

This is a simple, straightforward worksheet that allows people to organize their messages and results in a way that is easy to digest. First, they are asked to think about the practices that are more im-portant and less important to the effective performance of their jobs. Some feedback reports provide this information. In other cases, people must make the best determination they can, based on their understanding of their jobs and the environment in which they work. This first assessment of importance provides the context for setting priorities, once development needs have been identified.

Next, people are asked to review their data and any notes they may have made to identify apparent strengths and weaknesses. Al-though recipients can use whatever level of detail they choose, we find it is more helpful to indicate specific behavior items rather than just to note a practice. To refer to a strength or weakness as "I en-courage frank and open discussion of a disagreement" rather than just "teambuilding" is more likely to lead to action.

In addition to identifying strengths and weaknesses, we also ask people to indicate areas that are in need of further clarification, since they are bound to have questions about their data. This sec-tion of the consolidation worksheet will help prepare recipients for

Exhibit 8.1. Sample Feedback Consolidation Worksheet

Summarize your key strengths, weaknesses, and areas for clarification
on the chart.

	More Important	Less Important
Strengths	**A** Key Strengths *Supporting—being patient with complicated instructions; offering assistance with problems* *Teambuilding—encouraging cooperation to get work done* *Recognizing—praising improvements in performance; explaining why performance is good*	**D** *Planning—detailed project planning; analyzing ways to improve efficiencies* *Clarifying—explaining expected results and responsibilities on projects*
Weaknesses	**B** Development Targets *Problem Solving—making quick analyses of problems; handling work-related problems decisively; dealing with disruptions faster* *Consulting—getting people's reactions prior to making changes that affect them* *Inspiring—describing a vision for how we can all work together to accomplish a goal or task*	**E** *Informing—promptly informing people about decisions that affect their work* *Monitoring—consistently checking work projects against plans*
Areas for Clarification	**C** *Networking—forming alliances with people outside the work unit*	**F**

a constructive and focused discussion with the people who gave them their feedback.

Preliminary Identification of Development Targets

Before initiating a meeting with the raters or preparing a detailed development plan, recipients need to cull the data to focus on the critical few things that will make the greatest difference in their performance. As part of this process, we recommend that managers use a set of questions to help them move from the consolidation worksheet to a short list of preliminary development targets. (We say preliminary, because we believe it is important for people to validate their findings back on the job before preparing their development plans or taking other action.)

We begin by asking managers to focus on their strengths. Unfortunately, many people become so preoccupied with their weaknesses that they lose sight of what they already do that makes them effective. Our experience has shown us that the most effective managers not only clarify their development needs and remedy them but also get very clear about their strengths and how to leverage them in different situations. For behaviors that are important and seen as strengths, we ask people to think about the following questions:

1. In what kinds of situations does this strength serve you well?

   For example: Supporting—when the work is difficult and people are frustrated; when my expertise is needed by others

   Teambuilding—when a group is coming together to achieve a goal

   Recognizing—when coaching team members on new skills and recognizing improvements in performance

2. In what situations might this strength be less useful?

   For example: Supporting—working with people who are very experienced

Teambuilding—a team that is highly motivated and cohesive

*Recognizing—when I am the new person in the group and have less
credibility or do not know the appropriate form of recognition*

3. What steps could you take to leverage these strengths?

*For example: Supporting—be available especially to new team
members and ensure that I continue to develop my listening skills*

*Teambuilding—model cooperation and teamwork; ensure proactive
communication*

*Recognizing—ensure that my praise is specific; be sure to recognize
everyone*

In his role as facilitator, David DeVries encourages feedback recipients to use their strengths to address their weaknesses. He tells a story about one individual who used his incredible ability to problem solve and execute solutions to mend the fractured interpersonal relationships that were his main problem area. "The challenge for him," says DeVries, "was to accept these relationships as worthy of his attention and to accept his role in their 'brokenness.' Once he did so, he used his strengths to attack this area with great intensity."[2]

Changing behavior is difficult and requires a real commitment on the part of the individual. When identifying areas for development, therefore, it is important to be sure that the effort is worthwhile, that is, that the skill in question is directly related to effectiveness. The questions that follow serve two purposes: they help confirm that the target is worth pursuing, and they provide the basis on which to build a development plan. The following example is for Problem Solving.

• Why is it important to do this differently? How will it help me
be more effective (or successful, or satisfied with my job)?

*For example: Our work environment is changing. The pace is
increasing. We need to respond to our clients faster. Our*

> *department's role in providing direct service to clients has changed—we are now more visible.*

• What gets in the way of my doing it?

> *For example: I'm concerned that I am not getting the full picture or have enough information before I make a decision. I'm concerned that I am making a decision that will be inadequate.*

• How might I overcome these barriers?

> *For example: Practice on a small problem (not a big risk). Get input from a peer who does problem solving well. Talk to my boss about how my past decisions would have changed if my approach had been different. Speak to my mentor for a different perspective.*

• How can I use my strengths to help me?

> *For example: Ask the teams I work with to help with the analysis or help me understand when enough is enough. Ask team members to support me in taking what may feel like premature actions.*

• How can I minimize my risk when starting a new practice or using a new behavior?

> *For example: Start with a small problem. Use the team or do a joint project with a peer. Warn my boss of my attempt to change my approach and ask to get immediate feedback on decisions.*

The final set of questions helps managers confirm what they need to clarify before they finalize these preliminary findings and determine appropriate next steps. For this part, we ask participants to consider three questions:

• What parts of the feedback do I find confusing, incomplete, or contradictory?

> *For example: Networking—there are conflicting messages about the frequency with which I make contacts outside the department*

- Who could help me understand this better?

    For example: My boss's feedback indicates that he sees that I have a tendency to stay within the department, while direct reports see me differently.

- When will I meet with these raters (or others)?

    For example: I have set a meeting with my boss and will discuss it with him then. I will talk to my direct reports about this during my sharing and clarifying meeting.

This preliminary assessment of the data provides the basis for the next follow-up activity—the sharing and clarifying meeting. Up until now, participants' assessments may have been based on their interpretations alone. Many questions may be left unanswered, or findings may need clarification. Before development goals are finalized, it is useful for recipients to validate and confirm their findings.

The Sharing and Clarifying Meeting

Whenever possible, we encourage people to take the feedback back to the raters and share and clarify the results with them. Several benefits can be gained from discussing the feedback, in a constructive way, with the people who gave it or with members of the respondent group such as colleagues and direct reports, even if they did not complete a questionnaire. First, the discussion both confirms the recipient's hypothesis and provides information about how to act on the feedback. Second, it sends a message that the feedback was taken seriously and that the recipient intends to use it for personal development. Third, this type of discussion demonstrates to the raters that giving and getting feedback is accepted in the organization, while providing an opportunity for recipients to model the behavior they would like to see in others.

Raters may be uncomfortable about sitting down with the recipient and talking about the anonymous feedback they gave. However, it is important to inform all those involved, right at the beginning of the 360° process, that sharing and clarifying feedback are important parts of the follow-up process. Raters should be made aware that people may come back to them with general questions, once they have received their feedback. To allay their anxieties, it should be made clear to them—and to the recipients—that the discussion is supposed to focus not on their specific responses but on their reaction to the recipient's analysis (did he or she "get it"?) and on themes that are unclear. One tip: it should be made very clear that the sharing and clarifying session will not be used as an opportunity to identify or to get even with people who have given surprising or critical feedback.

The session may be conducted in a group or with each respondent individually. Some people feel that one-on-one meetings allow people to speak more freely. Others believe a group setting makes people more comfortable and encourages discussion. We believe the feedback recipient is in the best position to determine which approach will yield the best results with the individuals he or she chose as raters.

Whether the feedback is shared in a group or one-on-one, we strongly recommend that the recipient not share the entire report. One manager we worked with decided to copy his twenty-five-page report and send it to his colleagues with a cover note asking for their reactions. As he tells it, one colleague threw it out without even looking at it; one said he'd prefer to have a meeting; the third sent it back with a note that read, "You are in desperate need of help—good luck!"

The closest analogy we can think of is inviting friends over to see slides of your vacation. You find the slides fascinating and want to show every mountain, tree, and bird to relive your experiences. For your friends, however, the evening amounts to a tedious walk through a series of meaningless scenes. The same is true with feedback reports. We suggest, therefore, that people share only the main messages and themes they got out of the data, in order to test whether or not they "got it."

To illustrate the value of these sharing and clarifying meetings, let us consider the following example, taken from a feedback recipient's actual experience. This manager's respondents indicated that informing behaviors were used frequently, but they also recommended that these behaviors be used more.

At first, such a response appears contradictory—how much more can someone use a behavior that is already employed frequently? At the sharing and clarifying meeting, however, the manager learned that the weekly reports she had decided not to circulate because people were complaining about being overloaded with paper were the very documents they most wanted to see. She also discovered that people were actually pleased with the frequency and content of her informing behaviors but wanted to send a strong message to keep on that way, especially since the organization was undergoing major changes.

Sample Meeting Agenda

Probably the best way to make recipients feel comfortable about a sharing and clarifying meeting is to provide them with suggestions for making the meeting successful and give them an opportunity to rehearse what they will say. During our 360° feedback workshops, after managers have analyzed and consolidated their feedback and identified preliminary strengths and weaknesses, we provide a set of action steps for an effective sharing and clarifying meeting. These steps include:

1. Express appreciation. Thank the group for providing anonymous feedback, and describe how the feedback was useful.

2. Give an overview. Provide a summary of your strengths and areas for development, as perceived by the group.

3. Ask for input. Ask for the group's input on the areas you have identified, and then offer your ideas.

4. Discuss issues for clarification. Ask the group to help you understand feedback you found surprising or confusing.

5. Summarize next steps. Commit to actions you will take based on the feedback, and ask for people's help if appropriate.

6. Ask for ongoing feedback. Invite the group to let you know how you are doing, and set a follow-up date.

After reviewing the action steps, participants are shown a video model of an effective sharing and clarifying meeting, one that leads to a better understanding of the feedback without making people uncomfortable or violating the confidentiality agreement.

In-Class Rehearsal

Participants have an opportunity to think through and develop a plan for their sharing and clarifying meeting. A worksheet like the one shown in Resource A[3] provides people with guidelines and a framework for planning the meeting.

With their meeting plans in hand, participants are given an opportunity to rehearse what they will say and how they will say it. Many people find these rehearsals particularly helpful, because they get to hear how others react to their comments in a low-risk environment. Based on the feedback they receive, they make modifications to their plans. Like other skill-practice activities used in the group work session, this gives people a chance to get immediate feedback on their performance, minimizes the awkwardness of trying new behaviors, and enhances their confidence in their ability to conduct a constructive discussion about their feedback without making raters feel threatened or defensive.

If a person is quite sure he or she understands the feedback and knows how it should be incorporated into a development plan, is a follow-up meeting still necessary? The answer is "yes." Clarifying the feedback is not the only purpose of the meeting. The input of others can be very useful to determine the specific actions that would be most appropriate to address development needs or to help monitor progress. The sharing and clarifying meeting is an ideal time to ask for additional input and assistance from direct reports, peers, and bosses. This will also build the commitment of the raters to both the feedback process and the individual's development goals.

Right after people leave a feedback session or workshop, they usually have a high level of commitment to sharing the feedback and putting together their development plans. However, the meeting back at the office often does not occur immediately, and some of that enthusiasm may be lost or dissipated when the pressures and responsibilities of the job once again come to the forefront. The help of a human resource professional, boss, or mentor may be required to refocus the manager on the follow-up meeting. Acting as coaches, they can remind the recipient of the objectives of the follow-up meeting and offer advice on how to conduct it.

Creating a Development Plan

Once people have a clear picture of what their development goals are, it is time to look at how they will reach them. This will largely depend on the individual's personality and the specific areas he or she wants to develop. It is useful, however, to consider the strategies for change that have proved successful for others in the past.

Common Tactics of Successful Learners

The first question to ask is, "How do I learn and grow?" We all have our own personal tactics for learning new behaviors that we have developed and gotten used to over time. Therefore, each person needs to identify his or her own approach to learning before undertaking a specific action step toward development. Although these preferred learning methods will often be the centerpiece of the development plan, recipients need to be open to other approaches that may be more effective for learning a particular skill or behavior. For example, we may prefer to read about a subject to get more familiar with it. This works very well for knowledge-based development targets, but it may not be as appropriate for developing negotiating skills. Reading can be helpful, but the best way to develop this skill is to practice it and learn from experience.

A list of tactics used by successful learners, compiled by the Center for Creative Leadership,[4] follows:

1. Building new strengths or testing present strengths in new situations

2. Teaching someone else how to do something

3. Compensating for a weakness (for example, hiring someone to take care of detail if one is poor at doing so oneself)

4. Constructing strategies for learning (for example, imagining what things could look like in the future, examining the past for similar events, planning a series of activities to try, mentally rehearsing how one will act before going into problem situations, asking what the ideal manager or professional would do)

5. Action learning: taking action in order to ferret out real problems and increase learning; putting oneself in a situation where one must overcome or neutralize a weakness; emulating the behavior of an admired person

6. Enhancing self-awareness through feedback on strengths, weaknesses, and limits

7. Taking nonobvious choices and trying new behavior to overcome habits

8. Asking, "What lessons have I learned?"

9. Developing many flexible rules of thumb that can be applied in different types of situations

10. Analyzing successes as well as failures and mistakes

11. Seeking help in structuring learning (for example, seeking role models, keeping a learning diary, having dinner with those who have faced similar challenges, talking with previous job incumbents, attending courses, getting on-the-job tutoring)

12. Avoiding abstractions and generalities (for example, the way to develop people is . . .) and focusing on applying learning in specific situations

13. Searching for historical parallels that provide comparison points (for example, thinking of a good teambuilder to compare oneself with, comparing a time when one was strategic with one's present behavior)

14. Thinking about one's feelings and attitudes about a learning event

15. Asking oneself lots of questions

Strategies for Change

In our feedback work sessions, we cover five distinct self-development strategies, which we explain next in depth.

Reading. There are hundreds of books, journals, magazines, and newspapers related to the field of management and leadership. Recipients should also keep in mind the value of reading things that are not directly related to business but may nonetheless illuminate management and leadership issues. Works on figures like General George Patton and Sir Winston Churchill can be useful for understanding strategic and tactical thinking. Or science fiction might inspire managers to think creatively—to see the familiar in new ways and to approach it differently.

A useful resource for managers seeking to develop a specific behavior is *The Successful Manager's Handbook: Development Suggestions for Today's Managers*, published by Personnel Decisions, Inc. This book gives an overview of potential aids, from books to seminars, that managers can use for a wide variety of behavioral change and skill-development needs.

Self-monitoring. A tracking system helps recipients keep tabs on their progress. This approach does not require outside assistance. First, recipients need to decide which skill or behavior they want to concentrate on. It is best to select one that is directly relevant to their jobs but that they do not use very much at present. Examples of behaviors that are well suited to self-monitoring are Informing, Consulting, Monitoring, Recognizing, and Supporting.

Next, they should select several concrete and relevant examples of this skill or practice. Most feedback reports include specific examples of behavior. They may select all the examples from the

category, or, if they wish, identify other examples that are more relevant to their jobs and add them to the list. It is best to have between four and six behavior examples.

A self-monitoring checklist such as the one shown in Exhibit 8.2
can be used to list the behavior examples they want to monitor.[5] The
form shows the days of the week in columns, and the checklist is
good for a period of six weeks. Either during the day or at the end of
the day, the manager should make a check mark when he or she uses
one of the behaviors. Ideally, each behavior should be used at least
once per week, if appropriate. (No behavior should be overused,
however, or used for its own sake.) At the end of each week, recipients review their performance and determine how well they did.
They should be encouraged to congratulate themselves whenever
they attain their goals.

After a period of six weeks, the recipient will probably find that
he or she is using the practice naturally, without conscious planning. When this happens, it is time to switch to another practice
needing improvement and use the same procedure. If it is not too
confusing, recipients can use self-monitoring for more than one
managerial practice at a time. However, it is not a good idea to work
on more than three practices at a time.

Coaching-Consulting-Mentoring.   Recipients should identify someone who is qualified and willing to provide instruction and guidance
in the use of the skills and behaviors they want to improve.

Not all behaviors lend themselves to improvement by self-monitoring. If the successful use of a practice requires skills that the
manager currently lacks, coaching may be necessary. When a manager is already using a behavior, but with mixed success, a competent coach can provide advice on how to use it more effectively
and, if necessary, demonstrate or model its proper use.

The first step is to identify someone who is qualified to provide
coaching and likely to take the time and effort to help. This might
be the recipient's boss, a trusted colleague, or a management development specialist in the organization. Coaching is only feasible if

Exhibit 8.2. Self-Monitoring Checklist

Managerial Practice: _____

Behavior Example	Week 1					Week 2					Week 3					Week 4					Week 5					Week 6				
	M	T	W	TH	F	M	T	W	TH	F	M	T	W	TH	F	M	T	W	TH	F	M	T	W	TH	F	M	T	W	TH	F

someone is able and willing to provide the instruction, advice, and guidance needed.

Next, the manager must decide how best to approach this person and persuade him or her to help. An appropriate setting and time for the coaching to take place should be established, taking into account any special resources that may be needed and any other people whose cooperation is required. (Sometimes, it is possible to have direct reports provide feedback on a manager's use of certain practices.)

Management Training. When appropriate, a formal course, workshop, or seminar should be found that includes training in the relevant skills. If nobody with the skill and the time to provide appropriate coaching is available, formal training is an alternative approach. It is especially appropriate for learning complex skills that may not be easily acquired through occasional coaching, for learning conceptual and analytical skills such as those required for planning and problem solving, and for learning complex interpersonal skills such as those involved in mentoring. Classroom learning works best when it is directly related to the individual's real-life needs.

Once the recipient has identified a skill or behavior that he or she would like to improve with formal training, the next step is to identify an appropriate training opportunity. Many workshops and courses are available for practices such as planning, problem solving, clarifying, consulting, delegating, mentoring, and teambuilding. However, for some practices (inspiring, risk taking), it may be more difficult to find an appropriate training opportunity.

Participants should conduct a search of available training courses, including those within their own organizations, those in nearby colleges and universities, those offered by professional associations, and those offered by consulting companies. Before making a final decision, it is a good idea to probe beneath the superficial description presented in a catalogue or training brochure to determine whether the needed skills are indeed taught in a particular course or workshop.

The trainer or sales representative, for example, should be asked to explain exactly how the course or workshop improves the skills in question and what kind of opportunity will be provided to practice them during the course.

Finally, managers should consider combining training with self-monitoring or coaching; such an approach often proves especially effective.

Job Assignments. Feedback recipients can often find a way to enhance their current jobs (special projects, new challenges) or change assignments to provide them with developmental experiences.

Confirming the old adage that experience is the best teacher, research has shown that the most effective classroom is the job itself. In *The Lessons of Experience* and several studies conducted by the Center for Creative Leadership, executives reported that nearly half the events that had a lasting effect on their ability to manage were job assignments. Both new jobs and current jobs with intentionally constructed challenges are critical for continual learning, growth, and change.[6]

The following are the key learning experiences identified from the Center's research:

- *Scope assignments* include a huge leap in responsibility, moving into an unfamiliar line of business, or being switched to a line management position from a staff job. In these and other examples, managers are faced with bigger-scale, bottom-line accountability and the need to practice new skills or knowledge, such as leading direct reports and learning new technical skills.

- *Scratch assignments* include building something from nothing and taking action in the face of uncertainty. Managers are challenged to stand alone, make quick decisions, and find talented people for their staffs.

- *Fix-it assignments* include positions where an organization is in trouble, and things need to be turned around. These complex situations require managers to persevere, make decisions, and manage staff in a (sometimes) tough way.

- *Project or task force assignments* are short-term and highly visible and often require managers to work in areas where they have little or no content knowledge. Managers are tested in areas such as decision making, communicating, and establishing relationships.

- *A move from a line to a staff assignment* (in areas such as planning, finance, and administration) requires managers to learn new technical skills on the job, as well as appreciate the importance of influencing others where they have no direct authority.

- *Demotions, missed promotions, and unchallenging jobs* can also be learning experiences, although no one would seek them out. They teach humility and challenge managers to persevere and take stock of themselves.

Use of a Development Plan

Once the feedback recipient has identified a clear set of development targets, clarified his or her preferred learning techniques, and determined the most effective strategies for change, all the information should be consolidated so that he or she can refer back to it easily to refocus or clarify an objective. In our experience, a development plan is the best tool for this sort of consolidation. Not only will it serve as a reference and reminder, but the process of planning specific action steps forces people to think through all their development activities and how they can be monitored.

As part of our 360° work sessions, therefore, we include a planning guide that each person completes after the sharing and clarifying meeting (see Exhibit 8.3). The planning guide prompts the person to think about self-development in concrete terms, that is, "What will this development goal look like when I reach it?" "How will I get there?" "What resources will I need?" Answering these

Exhibit 8.3. Sample Development Goal Worksheet

DEVELOPMENT GOAL

Area for Development: Problem Solving

1. Developmental Goal: Improve speed with which I analyze
                          problems and make decisions

2. Criteria for Success: • Quality of solutions remains high
                            • Continue to do high-quality analysis
                            • Team members, boss, and peers will
                              recognize the increase in the speed and
                              greater flexibility of my decision making

3a. Typical Strategy: b. Actions/Next Steps:

   Coaching   1. Meet with Paul (mentor) next week to
                                  get ideas on his approach to dealing
                                  with frequent changes in his department.
                                  Review what he does, how he does it.
                                  Ask him about his biggest mistakes and
                                  what he learned from them.
                               2. Agree on a timetable to get coaching
                                  (meet at least twice within next month).

4a. Additional Strategies: b. Actions/Next Steps:

   Job assignment   1. Volunteer for the Delta Task Force
                                  (requires solution in a tight deadline;
                                  provides a complicated problem).
                               2. Work with team members to review
                                  issues and suggest alternative ways of
                                  analyzing information.
                               3. Get feedback from Linda (task force
                                  member) on problem-solving skills—find
                                  out what I do well and where I can
                                  improve!

   Reading   Read Managerial Decision Making
                               by George Huber and complete this
                               book by the end of next month.

questions focuses people's thinking about their development and builds enthusiasm for reaching the target.

Other planning guides ask similar questions of the manager. Whatever planning guide you use, it should include the following:[7]

1. A clear, written statement of the specific development goal

2. The standards to be used for measuring when the target has been successfully reached

3. The change strategies that will be incorporated into the plan

4. The action steps and learning techniques that correspond to each change strategy

5. The people who will be resources in the implementation or monitoring of the plan

Writing up the plan or keying it into a computer can serve to heighten its importance in the person's mind. If someone is working with a coach or mentor, that individual should get a copy as well; having another person aware that the manager is working toward specific goals increases the likelihood that those goals will be met. If the plan and the progress that has been made are periodically reviewed with a coach, it can really help to keep the manager focused and motivated.

Brooklyn Union Gas uses a 360° feedback survey with their high-potential managers. The training and development manager was faced with the challenge of ensuring that development plans were created and used without appearing to be a watchdog or policeman. He realized that it would be difficult for some people to use their bosses as coaches, given the nature of that relationship and the possible sensitivity of the feedback. The organization's formal mentoring program, however, assigned someone to act as a coach to each high-potential manager during the formative years of his or her career. So, the training and development manager decided to require all high-potential managers, within two weeks of receiving their feedback, to meet with their mentors to review the results and the development plan. To ensure that this meeting occurred, mentors were told to expect a call or to initiate the contact themselves.

Monitoring Progress

Because people feel more motivated to persist in their efforts if they experience a series of successes, the process of changing behavior should be defined in terms of a series of milestones along the way. That way, change targets can be pursued in manageable increments rather than asking people to make giant leaps. The milestones should be identified in terms of achieving goals, such as finishing a management development book or seminar or completing a challenging assignment. The following list of pointers can be distributed to help people stay on track:

- Keep your development plan on your computer, in your in-box, or in your mail folder; consult it frequently.
- Contract with your boss and coworkers. Describe to them the change you want to make, and ask them to give you ongoing feedback.
- Use family members as sources of feedback.
- Use calendar or project planning software to remind yourself of your commitment to change and the actions you have laid out for yourself.
- Review your analysis of barriers to change and determine ways to stay the course.
- Choose a trusted colleague and ask for help.
- Distribute the 360° feedback questionnaires to the same people (or as many as possible) twelve to sixteen months later. Compare your results to the benchmark that you established the previous time you received 360° feedback.

Additional Follow-up Activities

The following techniques serve both as a reminder of the skills to be practiced and as a motivator to use them successfully.

Follow-up Alumni Meeting. This option involves reconvening the recipients after a period of time (three to six months) to determine progress and discuss the problems they have encountered in meeting their development targets. The focus of the session should be on action plans and successes and failures; it allows people to learn from each other and reaffirm their commitment to their development targets.

Productivity Measures. This option involves monitoring hard performance data over a period of time to determine the impact of someone's behavior on the results and the deliverables for which that individual is responsible. This is the most powerful way to demonstrate the link between behavior change and results, but it is appropriate only when there is a clear, definable connection between the behavior of the individual and productivity measures. Given the complex nature of work processes and work relationships, such is not often the case.

Links to Formal Human Resource Management Systems

For 360° feedback to be seen as something more than just another fad, follow-up must occur at the organizational as well as the individual level. Specifically, the feedback process will need to be linked to existing human resource management systems in order to ensure that individuals' data are used for continuing learning and growth. Ideally, this means incorporating the feedback not only into training and development processes but also into appraisal, succession planning, and compensation systems. If managers know that they will be rewarded according to the progress they make toward reaching their development goals, they will be doubly motivated to translate their feedback into action.

In addition, linking the feedback to human resource systems can further organizational goals in various ways. We have already seen how the feedback process can contribute to achieving business strategy and to clarifying the selection criteria for particular jobs. Similarly, it can make individual managers more useful to the organization. If, for example, someone requests a job assignment change in order to achieve a development goal identified during the feedback process, the growth experience that results is likely to leave the manager more prepared to take on different roles within the organization. By broadening their scope and range, managers also broaden their usefulness.

Concluding Remarks

Ideally, the feedback people receive should continue to resonate and provide motivation for change not only in their current jobs but in their future jobs as well. Even when the formal follow-up comes to an end, learning can continue, and people can be actively engaged in trying to develop the skills that require improvement. As noted earlier, such life-long learning is a key factor in the success achieved by top executives. In organizations where continual learning is part of the corporate culture, the insights gained from 360° feedback become integrated into people's ongoing development.

Chapter Nine

Enhancing Performance Management Systems

Organizations exist to allow ordinary people to do
extraordinary things.

—*Ted Levitt*

Our primary focus in the previous chapters has been on the what, why, and how of multi-source feedback—what it is, why organizations use it, and how you can be sure people get the most out of the experience. Our focus in this chapter will be on how multi-source feedback can be integrated into the systems and processes organizations use to manage their human resources. We will show how the 360° process can enhance systems' effectiveness and ensure that the best possible decisions get made.

Although terms may vary from company to company, most organizations have human resource management (HRM) systems for planning, selection and placement, appraisal, development and training, and compensation. HRM systems are managed to align with and facilitate corporate or business unit objectives and strategies. While the subsystems of these components may have unique elements, the processes and structures of one system are likely to influence or be the source of information for another.

Attempts to integrate 360° feedback into these systems and processes can meet with significant hurdles. As organizations explore the possibility of using 360° feedback to enhance HRM systems, we predict that many will be disappointed when they learn that merely applying the technology is not sufficient for successful results. They may not have clarified how 360° feedback can contribute to each

HRM system or determined the role 360° feedback will have in the decisions that are made about employees. If their current HRM systems are weak or poorly implemented, multi-source feedback will not make them better. On the other hand, if their current systems are working well, they may be disappointed that the feedback has not made an immediately noticeable difference.

In this chapter, we will discuss the role 360° feedback can play in aligning three key components of a human resource management system—development and training, appraisal, and compensation—with organizational objectives. We will review both potential problems and the steps you can take to avoid them.

Benefits of Using 360° Feedback in Human Resource Decision Making

What follows is a list of benefits from discussions with practitioners who have successfully implemented 360° feedback as part of their human resource systems.

Provides a Common Model of Effective Behaviors and Performance Measures

Any good 360° feedback process is built from a competency model for effective performance. (As noted earlier, you will want to make sure that any instrument you use—whether developed in-house, purchased from a vendor, or purchased and then customized to meet the organization's needs—accurately reflects the values and success factors of your company.) This model, along with organizational objectives, allows you to establish performance measures that provide consistency and continuity to the decision making required for human resource management. For example, the list of job skills and requirements used to recruit people for certain jobs as part of the selection and placement process would be the same as or similar to the list used in the training and development process to target individual professional development needs. Likewise, when people's performance is evaluated, the same competencies would be emphasized. The use of a common model eliminates confusion about what it takes to succeed in an organization, helps people focus on the behaviors and results that are really important to the future of the company, and ensures that management is comparing "apples to apples" when making personnel decisions.

Ensures That Balanced, Objective Information Is Collected

Surveys at organizations using 360° feedback as part of assessment show that multi-source assessments are perceived as more fair, accurate, credible, valuable, and motivational than single-source evaluations. Thus, not only does 360° feedback enable management to make higher-quality decisions about an individual's performance, potential, and development needs, it also increases acceptance of appraisal decisions by those being evaluated.[1]

Supports and Reinforces Individual and Organizational Development Objectives

When people leave a 360° work session, they are frequently left on their own to pursue their development objectives. It is not uncommon for people to lose focus and momentum once they go back to dealing with the daily pressures of their jobs—some of which may be a contributing factor to their current behavior patterns and performance. Nor is it always possible for managers to secure the job assignments or special projects necessary for their development, since they may lack the influence or authority to arrange such things. When 360° feedback is integrated into HRM systems, however, the individual has a ready forum and many opportunities to discuss his or her needs and take appropriate next steps. At the same time, the organization gains insight and information that will help ensure that the right people are placed in the right positions at the right time.

Development and Training Systems

The purpose of most development and training systems is to identify the development needs of employees through formal and informal methods and to establish plans to address those needs, taking into account the company's strategic direction or the business unit's objectives. Many organizations provide a range of opportunities for individuals to gain insight into their strengths and weaknesses beyond the traditional career review or appraisal meeting. Typical offerings include assessment centers, workshops, and seminars where individuals can learn about their capabilities in a confidential setting. While they may not be required to share their results, most people return to their jobs with a clearer sense of their needs and seek the help of their boss or others to set development plans and determine appropriate next steps. In addition, many organizations offer a curriculum of courses, encourage special projects or assignments, and provide mentoring or coaching to help employees learn new skills and gain the knowledge required to perform their jobs better.

What Is Wrong with the Traditional System?

Even in organizations where there is a high level of satisfaction with existing development and training systems, there are usually one or two areas people would like to see improved. Cited next are the most common complaints from both human resource and line managers.

People are not clear about their development needs and improvement goals.

We recently ran a series of eight leadership development programs over a twelve-week period for the top 150 managers in a client organization. We began the program by asking people to talk about how they had prepared for the session and what their expectations for the two days were. About one-third of the attendees had held a meeting with their bosses to discuss what they wanted to get out of the program and why they were attending. While one-third of a group would usually be considered a low response rate, we were pleasantly surprised at how many people had prepared in some way for the program. More often than not, people attending such programs do not have a clear set of learning objectives or a sense of how a particular development experience will address their needs. And, in spite of the fact that they will spend hours or days away from the job on a quest to improve their performance, some people's choice of development opportunities has more to do with scheduling convenience than with any clearly identified need.

There is no focus on training priorities and allocation of training resources for the organization.

If you review an organization's catalogue of training programs, you will usually see an array of "basic skills" programs—time management, business writing, presentation skills—and "special need" programs—encouraging continuous improvement, customer focus, diversity training—that are added year to year in response to a particular challenge or crisis. Although the value of these programs is not in question, the issue becomes one of focus. What are the essential skills and knowledge needed to succeed in this organization now and in the future? What is the best use of limited training and development resources? What should be delivered in-house, and what should be addressed through external resources?

Other priorities get in the way of follow-up.

If, at the end of a workshop, someone can say what he or she learned or will do differently back on the job, most people would regard the program as successful. Unfortunately, most training and development events are free-standing—there is seldom any formal follow-up once participants return to work. Coupled with the fact that people often have no clear sense of why they are attending in the first place, the lack of follow-up makes it unlikely that the event will have any effect on their job performance.

The HRM systems don't "talk" to one another.

Valuable information about a person's strengths and development targets seldom flows from one system to another. Thus, an individual who could benefit from a special assignment or who is the perfect candidate for a vacant job in another part of the organization never surfaces in the placement system. In addition, when it is not integrated into other subsystems, traditional training can be somewhat haphazard—a string of events the individual engages in without any clear direction in mind.

How Feedback Can Enhance Development and Training Systems

The use of 360° feedback in development and training systems brings some distinct benefits to the individual and can help address many of the concerns discussed above. Specifically, it can:

Improve Personal Awareness and Clarify Expectations. When people learn how others perceive them, they become aware of what specific skills they need to develop and can therefore better choose the training and development experiences that will benefit them. Participating in a 360° feedback process and completing the self-report version of the questionnaire brings home to people which behaviors are most important. This increased clarity about critical success factors helps focus managers on relevant development goals.

Improve Decisions About Development Assignments. Because 360° feedback provides specific information about a person's strengths and weaknesses, an individual and his or her boss are better able to make informed decisions about appropriate job assignments or other opportunities for personal and professional growth. There is an increased likelihood that there will be a better fit of skill to task or task to development need than without the benefit of 360° feedback.

Clarify Training Priorities. Composite data on a representative sample of people can be used to determine the extent to which managers as a whole are actually using the behaviors identified as crucial to achieving the organization's business objectives. If current behavior is not consistent with expectations, training needs are illuminated, and a curriculum of courses can be designed with those needs in mind. To be really useful, group profiles should be based on a representative sample of the entire audience for training.

Monitor Progress. By using the first round of 360° feedback to establish a benchmark and then gathering the feedback again after a specific time has elapsed, it becomes possible to determine how much progress has been made toward achieving recipients' development targets.

Enhance Coaching Experiences. Because 360° feedback helps identify specific areas in need of development, it allows coaching interventions to become more focused.

Tips for Integrating 360° Feedback into Development and Training Systems

Integrating 360° feedback into your development and training systems is relatively easy and nonthreatening, since those who receive the feedback control who sees it and how it is used. Jay Strunk, manager of Training and Development at Zeneca Pharmaceuticals, has successfully overseen the process at his organization. As Strunk recalls, "We wanted the selection of training to be more thoughtful and based on clearly identified needs. At first, people were hesitant to get involved because they weren't sure that the feedback was really just for development. Once people realized that the data would not be used for evaluation, it was much easier to get them involved."[2]

Strunk began formally integrating 360° feedback with Zeneca Pharmaceuticals' training and development system about five years ago. When the system was first implemented, managers received 360° feedback on fourteen managerial practices using a generic questionnaire purchased from a vendor. After attending group workshops in which the feedback was presented and analyzed, meeting with their raters, and discussing their results with their bosses, Zeneca Pharmaceuticals' managers signed up for training programs that addressed their development needs.

Over a period of time, the comments collected from managers who participated in the 360° feedback process indicated that the fourteen managerial practices were not linked to the specific needs of Zeneca Pharmaceuticals' departments, nor were they owned by senior management. With the support of Zeneca Pharmaceuticals' president and his senior management team, a project team was formed to work with the lines of business to adapt and install a competency model that better described the behaviors required to achieve high performance, support Zeneca Pharmaceuticals' strategic direction, and meet the needs of the various departments. To support the team's efforts, Zeneca Pharmaceuticals' Training and Development group also developed half-day training modules for each of the twenty-four competencies that were identified.

To help managers understand how they are currently performing and to help them determine areas for continued development, Zeneca Pharmaceuticals' Training and Development group has developed a feedback questionnaire based on the five Core Competencies, as well as four others considered particularly vital for managerial high performance. As part of the implementation plan, the questionnaire was piloted with the president and his management team. "I've been pleased with the progress we've made so far," Strunk says. "The support we've been getting from the senior management team will give a boost to the process when we roll it out to the rest of the employees, and having our own competency model ensures our development efforts will focus on the skills and knowledge that really make a difference at Zeneca Pharmaceuticals."[3]

Despite this apparent ease of integration, several steps should be taken to ensure that the use of 360° feedback will lead to sound training and development decisions.

Start with a competency model that is linked to business performance.

Providing feedback on competencies that have been shown to correlate with superior work unit performance will increase people's interest in assessing the degree to which their skills match up against critical success factors. It will also motivate them to devote their time and energies to improving and developing skills that will have the greatest pay-off for the organization.

Establish a clear link between development opportunities and the critical competencies.

A curriculum of internal and external programs based on the skills, knowledge, and behaviors measured by the competency model will ensure that people's development efforts are relevant to organizational needs. The course catalogue might describe the contents of each course in terms of the competencies addressed, and internal trainers should be encouraged to use workshop examples that illustrate elements of the competency model. This alignment of curriculum offerings and competencies will also ensure that trainers and other staff resources are used effectively.

Ensure that the 360° feedback system has integrity.

When people perceive their feedback as fair, accurate, and credible, they feel more motivated to participate in relevant training and development events. As mentioned in previous chapters, if participants understand the model on which their feedback is based, the data collection process, and how to select raters they believe will provide useful information, they will be more inclined to trust their feedback, and thus to seek out training.

Encourage people to share feedback with their bosses and coaches.

Many people are reluctant to discuss the results of their feedback with their bosses, since they feel that this type of discussion is uncomfortably close to a performance appraisal. Some organizations avoid this problem by requiring that follow-up sessions take place with mentors, not bosses.

Although bosses may be instructed to use the information for development purposes only, not for performance appraisal, it is difficult to imagine that they will forget the 360° feedback at appraisal time. We therefore suggest that employees share only the conclusions that result from their analysis of the complete set of data— three or more key strengths, three development targets, and one or two areas that need further clarification. In this way, the employee is still in control of the information and only shares what he or she is comfortable discussing; the boss can serve as a coach and resource without violating the confidentiality of the feedback.

Monitor progress.

The first round of 360° feedback allows an individual to clarify current capabilities and establish a performance benchmark. Once development targets are established, people can monitor their progress by administering the 360° questionnaire nine to twelve months later, depending on the kind of information collected (improvement in some behaviors takes longer to become noticeable to others). This enables recipients or their organizations to collect hard data on progress toward achieving development goals.

Performance Management Systems

The question most frequently asked by both line managers and human resource professionals during our forums and presentations is, "Should we use 360° feedback for performance management?" By this, they usually mean, "How can multi-source feedback be used in our appraisal and compensation systems—what works, what doesn't, and why?" Although many organizations are interested in using 360° feedback to support appraisal and compensation systems, relatively few are actually doing it.

According to Mark R. Edwards, CEO of TEAMS, Inc., a consulting firm that specializes in multi-source feedback systems, nearly all the Fortune 1000 companies have experimented with 360° feedback for development purposes. However, when he surveyed a group of Fortune 1000 companies at the 1995 360° Feedback Users' Conference, none of his respondents' organizations had made a commitment to using 360° feedback for performance appraisal and compensation purposes.[4]

The issue of whether or not it is appropriate to use 360° feedback in performance appraisal is probably the most hotly debated question among experts in the field. Maxine Dalton, of the Center for Creative Leadership, is among those who have come out strongly against the idea. "My argument," she says, "has two main components: First, you aren't going to be successful in bringing about change if people resist their data, and by having the feedback administered as part of a process that affects their salaries and chances for promotion, you increase the likelihood that they're going to resist. Second, studies have shown that when raters believe others will be hurt by what they say, they aren't going to be as honest, so the quality of the data just won't be as good."[5] Dalton also cites a recent survey of organizations that used 360° feedback as part of their performance appraisal systems; over one-half of the companies surveyed had decided to stop using the feedback for that purpose.[6]

Gary Yukl, a noted expert in the fields of management and leadership, is also opposed to the idea of linking multi-source feedback to performance appraisal systems. "The type of specific behavior feedback most valuable for development is not necessarily useful for evaluation. In most types of managerial jobs, there are multiple paths to effective performance, and most behaviors are related to outcomes in a complex way. Moreover, behavior measures need to be more accurate when used for assessment than when used for developmental purposes, and I doubt whether any of the currently available instruments are accurate enough for assessment." Interestingly, Yukl goes on to say, "Appraisal by peers can pose problems when the raters are competitors for rewards or promotion—some raters may intentionally paint a very negative picture of a key competitor."[7]

Despite the questions associated with the method of data collection and the accuracy of the data, many companies continue to be interested in the possibility of using 360° feedback as part of their performance appraisal systems, and some who have done so found ways to avoid the pitfalls cited above. We will focus our discussion, therefore, on the potential advantages of the use of multi-source feedback in this context and offer some suggestions on how to minimize the potential difficulties that may arise.

Moving from the use of 360° feedback for development only to its use for appraisal and compensation is a big leap. There are two fundamental differences that make the transition difficult. The first concerns ownership of the data. In development-only systems, the data are the sole property of the recipients. They determine who sees them and control how they will be used. When 360° feedback is used in performance management systems, however, the data become the property of the organization. Who sees the data and how they will be used are determined by how the organization has defined the structure and process for performance management.

The second difference relates to the perception of what is at stake for the feedback recipient. In development-only systems, employees focus their efforts on enhancing their skills and improving how they contribute to work unit effectiveness. The organization supports their efforts, but unless development objectives are integrated into performance objectives, there is seldom any repercussion if personal development targets are not met. When 360° feedback becomes part of performance management systems, the situation changes dramatically. Now the data will be used to measure results and determine promotability and pay. Such decisions have a much greater effect on the individual than being told what training program to attend or what development initiatives to pursue. Because of this, employees want to be sure that the use of multi-source feedback will provide unbiased information and serve their interests as well as the organization's.

For the purpose of our discussion, we will look at the two components of performance management—appraisal and compensation—separately, beginning with appraisal.

Appraisal

A well-implemented appraisal system serves several purposes. First, it ensures that employees understand their overall roles and the specific objectives and goals by which they will be evaluated. Second, in the periodic reviews that are held to monitor progress toward these goals, people are provided with information on the extent to which they are on track and have a chance to discuss how to get back on target if necessary. During these reviews, which are likely to take place on a monthly or quarterly basis, goals may be adjusted due to changes in business conditions or strategy. Finally, a formal performance assessment is conducted to rate accomplishments over a previously agreed-upon time period (usually annually). The appraisal discussion will include an assessment of the employee's performance, and, in some organizations, will be followed by a discussion of career potential or areas for improvement.

What Is Wrong with Traditional Appraisal Systems?

A number of elements need to be in place for appraisal systems to work—understanding and agreement on performance goals, a process for collecting ongoing performance data, and a framework for productive periodic review and formal appraisal discussions. However, three factors serve as hurdles in this process—lack of agreement on performance criteria, our inability as evaluators to process a lot of information, and our need, when being evaluated, to preserve our self-image.[8] We will discuss these factors and then review how 360° feedback can be used to minimize their impact. Finally, we will provide guidelines for making 360° feedback work within an appraisal system.

Lack of Agreement on Performance Criteria. Anyone who has participated in a performance appraisal as either a boss or a direct report will not be surprised to hear that the two parties do not always agree on what it takes to perform the job effectively. Our own experience supports this conclusion. Part of the data we collect with our 360° instrument, "Compass: The Managerial Practices Survey," consists of importance ratings for the fourteen practices related to effective performance. The boss rates which practices he or she feels are essential for the direct report's effective performance of the job, and the direct report does the same. Their perspectives rarely coincide at every point.

If bosses and employees cannot come to an agreement on what is required for good performance, it is hardly surprising that they come to different conclusions about the employee's effectiveness in meeting performance goals. In addition, if the appraisal focuses only on the ability to accomplish goals or outcomes, without reviewing the behaviors required for successful performance, it does little to close this gap in perception or help the employee understand what changes are required for improvement.

The Inability to Handle Lots of Information. The thought process behind an effective appraisal is very complex. Experts break down the intricate process for collecting and processing information used in the appraisal process into observing behaviors, translating these observations into a cognitive representation, storing the representation in memory, retrieving the stored information, integrating the stored information with other data, and finally, assessing and evaluating the data.[9] One expert has concluded that the complexity of the process and the limitations on human information-processing capabilities often cause bosses and employees to simplify the task and work from overall impressions rather than specific details.[10] In other words, because each of us uses our own framework to process and remember information, we attach more weight to information that fits our model of the world and discount information that is inconsistent with that model. These different approaches to remembering and processing large amounts of information contribute to a potential lack of agreement between the employee and boss on the final evaluation.

Concern About Self-image.   For some people, appraisals can be an opportunity to reaffirm their value to the organization and celebrate their growth and accomplishments over the previous year. For others, appraisals can be extremely threatening—contentious, demoralizing, and anxiety-producing encounters that bring all the employee's defense mechanisms into play. Defense mechanisms protect our self-concept; as a result, we can generate a subjective and distorted view of our contributions or results. When people devote energy to denying or explaining away performance problems in order to preserve a positive self-image, agreement on the evaluation will be difficult.[11]

How 360° Feedback Can Enhance Appraisal Systems

As we have mentioned, you should not assume that the 360° system you use for development will be adequate for appraisal purposes. In considering the use of 360° feedback for appraisal, we strongly urge you to thoughtfully consider what data you will collect, from whom, and how. When used appropriately, however, 360° feedback can make a positive contribution to your appraisal system in several ways—by helping to gain agreement on expectations, by using a broader range of information, and by facilitating open discussion.

Gain Agreement on Expectations.   The addition of a 360° process can help minimize the differences in perspective by ensuring that the boss and direct report work from the same model of effective behaviors and outcomes. Comparing boss and direct report ratings of the importance of critical success factors and using these data as a springboard for discussing what it takes to succeed in a position can bring the two perspectives significantly closer together.

Use a Broader Range of Information.   The use of 360° feedback provides a more objective measure of a person's performance. Incorporating the perspective of multiple sources provides a broader view of the employee's performance and helps minimize biases that result from not only limited views of behavior but limited information-processing capabilities. In addition, because the results of a 360° process are usually documented in a report, there is less dependence on the boss's and employee's memory and retrieval mechanisms.

Facilitate Open Discussion.   Using 360° feedback can play an important part in keeping the employee open to the appraisal discussion. Studies have shown that people are more likely to modify their self-perceptions in the face of multi-source feedback.[12] Multiple views of a person's behavior also increase the likelihood that important elements of performance will not be overlooked or minimized, and a well-run appraisal meeting in which the boss provides balanced feedback in a constructive manner reduces the employee's defensiveness during the appraisal process.

Tips for Using 360° Feedback Successfully

If the decision has been made to use 360° feedback in a performance appraisal process, it is essential that the feedback be seen as only one component of the appraisal, not the entire basis for evaluation. People must receive information on what results were achieved, as well as how results were achieved. We believe 360° feedback is most effective in performance appraisal when it is used for goal setting, that is, during the part of the process that looks ahead rather than back. Recipients of the feedback should use it as the basis for a conversation with their bosses about strengths and development targets going forward. The development targets can then serve as the baseline from which progress toward desired levels of performance is periodically tracked.

Before we discuss how to make 360° feedback work in the appraisal system, we must offer two caveats. First, the information you collect and how you collect that information should be different for use in appraisals than for development. Second, the addition of 360° feedback will not fix a traditional appraisal system that is not currently working. Although 360° feedback can be used to address some of the issues related to fairness and accuracy, it will not ensure that people have open and honest discussions about the data and identify appropriate next steps.

The following guidelines and suggestions can help ensure that the use of multi-source feedback actually improves your appraisal process.

Involve People. Having recipients participate in various aspects of the appraisal process will strengthen their commitment to the overall process and increase their commitment to the decisions that get made. Have recipients jointly clarify performance expectations and set goals, ask them who should serve as raters (sometimes people outside the organization will be named), and give them an opportunity to review and interpret the results.

Ensure That Relevant Data Are Being Collected. Focus on behaviors and outcomes that raters are capable of observing and are competent to evaluate. This increases people's confidence in the quality of the data and their usefulness as part of the overall assessment. Such confidence is also increased by allowing people to participate in the selection of the raters who will evaluate them.

Ensure That No One Rater Can Affect the Outcome. Be sure to use a large enough sample or eliminate the highest and lowest scores to ensure that no one rater can skew the data.

Train Raters in What and How to Observe. The better people understand what to look for and how to record critical incidents that can be used as examples to support their ratings, the better the quality of the information that will be collected. Trained raters provide clearer, more detailed information that contributes to understanding the data and to developing effective plans for improvement.

Have Raters Support Their Evaluations. This suggestion is especially appropriate for high-performance or self-managed teams. We believe that, whenever possible, raters should discuss their observations and evaluations with other raters. Because of the complexity of the information processing required to arrive at an accurate assessment, the appraisal process benefits from discussion—what others say triggers thoughts and prevents selective memory. We also believe that raters should be required to provide a rationale for their rating to other raters. Such discussion not only enlightens others, it also highlights biases and prevents people from using the process to act on personal grudges.

Move Slowly and Start Small. We strongly recommend that any organization considering using 360° feedback in the appraisal process begin by using it for development only and gradually make it part of appraisal discussions with a pilot group. Even then, the focus should be on the goal-setting portion of the appraisal. People need to get comfortable with the idea of multi-source feedback as a development tool. They frequently benefit from experiencing the feedback process and gaining an appreciation for its objectivity. Once this hurdle has been overcome, there will be less resistance to the use of 360° feedback in broader appraisal discussions that include the evaluation itself.

Household International is an excellent example of an organization that has successfully integrated 360° feedback into its appraisal process. As a company, Household has always valued training and development as a way to enhance the quality of its workforce. The organization constructed a dedicated development center in

1992 and has been using 360° feedback as part of its development activities and programs for more than five years. In 1994, a change in top management precipitated a change in strategic direction and organizational values. Managers in the organization were now being asked to lead and manage in different ways. Household's senior management team wanted to be certain that people were clear about the new expectations and what values and leadership behaviors would be measured and rewarded. Steve Gonabe, vice president of training and development, was given the assignment of integrating Household's expectations, values, and critical leadership success factors into the discussions bosses conducted with their direct reports about their performance and their future with the company.

A straightforward system was developed, unencumbered by forms or paperwork. Each manager, starting with the top 120 people in the organization, received 360° feedback on the competencies that supported the new values and were required to achieve business objectives. A day-and-a-half work session was used as the forum to review the feedback and prepare people for meetings with their bosses to discuss their results and prepare business objectives and development targets for the following year. Because the process was started at the top of the organization, the expectation was established that these meetings would actually be held—nobody had to wonder, "Will my boss go through this process?" There was almost no resistance to the use of 360° feedback as part of this type of discussion, because the members of the organization were very 360° savvy, had confidence in the integrity of the data, and knew what to expect.

Should You Move to a Multi-rater Performance Appraisal System?

The following is a checklist to determine if your organization is ready to use 360° feedback as part of its performance appraisal system.

1. Have you been using 360° feedback for development only? Are people familiar with the multi-source feedback process and its advantages?

2. Do people have confidence in the integrity and confidentiality of your current 360° feedback process?

3. Have you analyzed your existing appraisal process to determine what about it works and what aspects need improvement? Can the weaknesses you identified be addressed by the addition of 360° feedback?

If you answered "no" to any of the above questions, your organization may not yet be ready for this step.

Compensation

As we have seen, moving from using 360° feedback for development only to using it to set goals during the performance appraisal process requires work but can be fairly straightforward. The next logical use for 360° feedback in the performance appraisal process is in the area of compensation. This particular transition, however, presents some distinct problems.

It has always been difficult to translate a numerical rating of performance into what is perceived as a fair pay increase. Adding multi-source ratings does not necessarily address this issue. To make an accurate assessment of performance that will be useful for decisions about pay, it is essential to evaluate not only what a manager does but also how the work gets done. Although 360° feedback works well for assessing management behavior and leadership competencies, it is not well suited to measuring work unit results. Raters may not have an opportunity to observe work unit outcomes or have access to the information necessary to determine if business performance targets have been achieved. Generally, it is the boss who is in the best position to make this type of assessment. So, a combination of 360° feedback and the boss's evaluation is required to get the complete picture necessary to make a decision about compensation.

The question then arises about how much weight should be given to the boss's evaluation and how much to the multi-source feedback. According to Mark R. Edwards, when most organizations first use 360° ratings in compensation decisions, they give them a moderate or no weighting and gradually evolve to 50 percent or higher. Edwards has identified several factors, based on nineteen years of research, that an organization should consider to determine when and if it is feasible to use 360° feedback for other purposes besides development. These factors include:[13]

1. *User satisfaction:* 75 percent of affected employees should strongly support the use of multi-source feedback in general.

2. *Spread of scores across performance measurements:* The range of scores should clearly differentiate high, medium, and low performance. If everyone appears to be a high performer, the system fails to provide enough information for pay and promotion decisions, because everyone looks alike.

3. *Valid and fair feedback:* Distinctions among people should represent truly high, medium, and low performance. Ratings must be based on actual performance and not on friendship, collusion, or competition, nor on gender, age, or ethnic background.

4. *Accountability for ratings:* Raters must be accountable for honest ratings. The percentage of invalid responses should be below 5 percent, and people who consistently provide invalid responses should be held accountable.

5. *Safeguards to ensure fairness:* People should understand and support safeguards that minimize scoring biases. Such safeguards include valid performance criteria, procedures for selecting competent and trustworthy raters, and a scoring method that eliminates clearly invalid responses.

Tips for Making 360° Feedback Work in Pay Decisions

In general, we believe that 360° feedback has a clear role to play in all aspects of the performance management system. There is little downside to its use for development or as part of goal setting and measuring progress toward achieving those goals. However, if an organization wants to incorporate 360° feedback into its compensation and promotion systems, it should consider the following caveats:[14]

- Use 360° feedback in combination with boss's evaluations of how well work unit performance targets were achieved.
- Multi-source feedback should initially be given low weight in the compensation decision until user confidence and support are established. Gradual increases in weight should parallel increases in user acceptance.
- Respondent anonymity must be assured, or scores will be inflated and generally useless.
- Time requirements should be kept to a minimum. If the data collection methodology is too time-consuming or cumbersome, raters may not be as thoughtful or complete when responding. Administration should be quick, convenient, and efficient.

What Is Required to Make It Work?

Sometimes, it seems as though every organization is hurrying to integrate 360° feedback into every human resource management system as soon as possible. And why not? Many organizations have experienced success using 360° feedback for development, so why not use it for appraisal and compensation? The systems are aligned. They should feed into each other. The data should be applicable in many ways. We believe the logic of this argument is sound, and the perception of 360° feedback's potential to enhance human resource management systems is also valid. There are, however, some conditions that need to exist if 360° feedback is to be used successfully in appraisal and compensation systems. These include:

A culture that supports open, honest feedback

Not surprisingly, 360° feedback works best in companies where the environment is participatory rather than authoritarian—where giving and receiving feedback are the norm and are seen as valuable sources of information. If the current system of supervisor-only feedback is not working due to a lack of straight talk and a hesitancy to give direct feedback, it is unlikely that adding additional sources of data will make it better.

Systems that minimize irrational responses and have built-in ways to identify people whose ratings are untrustworthy

For multi-source feedback to work, employees need to believe that the feedback is unbiased and objective. They need to have confidence in the intentions and credibility of the raters. In order to reach this point, the system should not reward individuals who abuse it, nor should it permit any single rater to carry too much weight.

Users who support the system and are willing to invest the time required to make it work

The addition of 360° feedback makes an already time-intensive appraisal process even more demanding for participants. With more data to collect and more information to sift through, employees must value the additional information, or they will not be willing to provide the data or properly use the available data. Herman Simon, a former plant manager at a Quaker pet food plant that had been using multi-source feedback as part of the appraisal process, describes a situation that illustrates the importance of this point. "In the early days, we put a fair amount of work into the appraisal process. When we started, people were honest and reasonably strict. After about ten years, it began to fall apart. Soon everybody was top-rated; everybody got good grades, unless somebody really stepped out of bounds."[15]

Clear and agreed-on performance measures and behaviors

When 360° feedback is being used for development only, the organization may be able to make do with a list of behaviors and skills that have reasonable face validity and general support. However, the stakes are much higher when 360° feedback is being used to determine pay and career paths. The results and behaviors for which people will be held accountable must be clear, unambiguous, specific, observable, and agreed to by those who will be measured. In addition, there should be equal focus on what (financial performance, new products, decreasing costs) was accomplished and how (leadership style, ethics, teamwork) it was accomplished. To build a culture of success, a company must be willing to say to its employees that it is not enough to hit the number—we care how you get there.

A sound 360° feedback process

The requirements and procedures of a highly credible 360° feedback process have been discussed at length in previous chapters, for example, the validity of the model and the way the data are collected and presented. Although all these aspects are relevant, two aspects of sound 360° feedback procedure are particularly important for use with appraisal and compensation systems—the validity and reliability of the practices on which people will be measured and the confidentiality of the raters' responses. If an organization is going to make pay and promotion decisions based on the feedback from a 360° instrument, it had better be quite certain that the instrument accurately and reliably measures what it claims to measure. And if an organization wants to ensure that the feedback is honest and accurately reflects what is observed on the job, it must protect the anonymity of all raters. Without this assurance, it is difficult to expect raters to be totally candid in their evaluations.

In Conclusion

As we hope this book has made clear, 360° feedback can be a powerful tool for organizational change. In a period of rapid and often bewildering environmental shifts, it helps organizations identify crucial success factors and align their internal competencies with the challenges they face. And in an era of increasingly horizontal management structures, it provides an opportunity to democratize the feedback process, bringing it in line with the changes in internal structure and culture that so many companies are setting in motion.

At the same time, like other powerful tools, multi-source feedback must be used appropriately and intelligently in order to be effective. When it is initiated for its own sake, with no clear goal in mind other than the desire to keep up with current trends, or when it is implemented clumsily, or without a broad base of support, the results are likely to be disappointing or even disastrous.

The recommendations and guidelines contained in this book are designed to help you avoid making such mistakes in your own organization. Our purpose in writing it has been to ensure that 360° feedback will not wind up being seen as just another fad that promised something it could not deliver.

That is why we have chosen to place so much emphasis on the importance of getting support for the process at all levels of the organization. In fact, if we could leave you with just one piece of advice for ensuring that 360° feedback works well in your organization, it would be this: Involve as many people as possible as early as possible. Getting input from stakeholders and decision makers throughout the organization will not only ensure that the 360° feedback initiative genuinely reflects their needs and concerns, it will also increase enthusiasm across the board and thus contribute enormously to the success of the process.

We have seen for ourselves just how effective multi-source feedback can be. Our work with a diverse group of companies has convinced us that organizations'—and individuals'—real strength lies in their capacity to bring about changes that maximize their potential. Our belief in the capacity for change has been continually reinforced by the transformations we have witnessed, and we hope that this book will help you make 360° feedback a positive force for change in your organization.

Examples of 360° Feedback

Leadership Practices Inventory: Assessing How Leaders Get Extraordinary Things Done

James M. Kouzes and Barry Z. Posner
in cooperation with
The Tom Peters Group/Learning Systems

The story of the development and use of the *Leadership Practices Inventory (LPI)*—our thirty-item, 360° behavioral assessment tool—is one of a journey from leadership myths to leadership measures. Motivated by a desire to demonstrate that leadership is something that can be observed in the broader population, we conducted a series of studies to determine what ordinary people did to get extraordinary things done. What this mountain of data conclusively and consistently demonstrates is that leadership is an observable, measurable, and learnable set of practices.

We discovered that exemplary leaders engage in five fundamental leadership practices:

Challenge the Process—Leaders *search out* challenging opportunities and *experiment* and take risks.

Inspire a Shared Vision—Leaders *envision* an uplifting and ennobling future and *enlist* others in a common vision.

For more information about this assessment tool, please contact James M. Kouzes or Barry Z. Posner, 555 Hamilton Avenue, Palo Alto, CA 94301.

Enable Others to Act—Leaders *foster* collaboration and *strengthen* others.

Model the Way—Leaders *set* the example and *achieve* small wins.

Encourage the Heart—Leaders *recognize* individual contributions and *celebrate* team accomplishments.

Since our research began more than fifteen years ago, we have reviewed more than sixty thousand completed *Leadership Practices Inventory* forms. By every measure, the LPI has sound psychometric properties. Internal reliabilities for the five leadership practices (both Self and Observer versions) are very strong and are consistent over time. The underlying factor structure has been sustained across a variety of studies and settings, and support continues to be generated for the instrument's predictive and concurrent validity.

More important, the LPI is not only for people in formal organizations, with bosses and direct reports. While the original *LPI-Self Analysis and Assessment* was designed for managers and the *LPI-Observer* for the person's immediate manager, direct reports, peers, and nondirects, more universal versions of the LPI are in use, including the *LPI-Student*, the *LPI-Individual Contributor*, and the *Team LPI*.

Another of the unique features of the LPI is that it does not have to be purchased from or scored centrally by a training or testing company. Because we believe that leadership is everyone's business, we developed an instrument that is available directly from either the instrument publisher—Pfeiffer & Co., an imprint of Jossey-Bass—or from the exclusive distributor of *The Leadership Challenge Workshop™*, The Tom Peters Group/Learning Systems.

From Assessment to Improvement: Using the LPI in Training and Development

While the LPI is used extensively in assessment centers and research projects, its most common use is for leadership development, and the most common format for development is a workshop. This experience typically involves prework, scoring, model overview, feedback, personal reflection and observation, practice, and application planning.

Prework and Scoring

At least two weeks prior to a leadership development workshop, participants receive a prework package that includes the LPI-Self and at least five LPI-Observer forms. To provide a safe environment for respondents and participants, the forms are usually distributed by a third party, most commonly an internal human resource development staff member or an external training provider.

The LPI can be self-scored or centrally scored. Since anonymity and data security are frequent issues, the completed LPI forms are usually returned directly to a program administrator for scoring. (While it is rarely used, a self-scoring option is available that puts the tool directly into the hands of the feedback recipient.)

The program administrator can either manually transfer Self and Observer ratings to the five practice grids or enter data into a computerized scoring program that performs all functions electronically. Once scoring is complete, the administrator prepares a confidential feedback report for each participant.

Model and LPI Overview

In workshop settings, facilitators present the Kouzes-Posner model before they distribute individual LPI feedback. The overview gives participants a context for interpreting their feedback and applying it to on-the-job situations. As an alternative to a live presentation, a video on *The Leadership Challenge*™ is available.

Following an overview, the program leader orients participants to the LPI feedback and briefly explains the origins of the instrument, reviewing these essential points:

1. The LPI is designed to measure exemplary leadership behaviors and practices that have been identified by Kouzes and Posner in their research as the actions that explain why leaders get extraordinary things done in organizations.

2. The LPI is not about attitudes and intentions but about actual behavior. It does not evaluate IQ, style, or personality. Neither does it measure broader management behaviors. It only measures leadership practices that were shown to be effective in the Kouzes and Posner research.

3. Each statement on the LPI measures one of the specific behaviors that make up one of the five leadership practices in the Kouzes-Posner model.

4. There are six behaviorally based items measuring each practice, for a total of thirty items.

5. Each statement asks respondents to indicate the extent to which the leader being assessed engages in that behavior on a scale ranging from 1 (rarely or seldom) to 5 (very frequently or almost always).

6. The LPI has passed all relevant statistical tests of reliability and validity. This means measurement errors are minimal, and correlation between practice and effectiveness is very strong.

With this background provided, the program leader then distributes the confidential feedback reports to each participant.

Feedback Display

If program sponsors have chosen the computer scoring option, the print-out that each participant receives provides seven pages of data. The first page summarizes the data by providing: (1) the self-rating on each of the five practices, (2) the mean score of ratings given by all observers for each practice, (3) the standard deviation for the observer ratings on each practice, and (4) the ratings given by each observer on each practice. Observer ratings remain anonymous and are coded as letters of the alphabet. The LPI computer scoring program, as well as the manual scoring, maintains respondent anonymity. An available option will cluster respondents by direct report, manager, peer, and other.

Exhibit A.1. Leadership Practices Inventory (LPI)

Profile for [Workshop Participant's Name]

Title of the Workshop
with name of trainer, company, etc.
Today's Date

	Self Rating	LPI-Observer Ratings		A	B	C	D	E
		Avg	Std Dev					
Challenging	25	20.6	3.4	22	24	16	24	17
Inspiring	16	18.6	3.9	23	16	18	23	13
Enabling	26	22.0	4.5	26	25	20	25	14
Modeling	27	22.6	3.4	25	26	18	25	19
Encouraging	22	21.4	2.4	23	23	19	24	18

Exhibit A.1. illustrates the summary feedback page.

The second page displays all thirty LPI items, from highest to lowest average observer scores. While the first page provides a summary by practice, this page provides an item-by-item summary. Because the items are ranked from most to least frequent, this display is useful for targeting specific behaviors for improvement.

The next five pages display self-ratings, mean scores, standard deviations, and respondent scores for each item in a practice.

If participants or sponsors have chosen to use the manual scoring option, grids and line graphs in the self-analysis guidebook are filled in by respondents during the workshop or by administrators prior to the event.

Feedback Review

It has been our experience that participants are anxious to quickly review their own feedback before the program leader guides them through a more thorough examination of the data. Consequently, program leaders distribute the confidential forms and allow people about five to ten minutes to quietly leaf through their data.

Once participants have skimmed their feedback sheets, program leaders walk the group through a page-by-page, item-by-item analysis of the data, using a "sample participant" LPI as a reference. Program leaders remind participants to look for *messages, not measures*. In particular, they direct people's attention to their own perceptions of what their strengths and weaknesses are and how far those perceptions are reflected in others' assessments. Any discrepancies between observer and self-ratings, along with any sharp variations among the observers themselves, should be noted and analyzed for possible causes. Finally, participants are asked to identify the three or four strongest messages they are getting about their leadership, as well as the one or two practices (three or four specific behaviors) they want to target for improvement.

Before concluding the LPI review, participants plot their self-ratings and observer averages on a percentile ranking graph. This grid allows participants to compare themselves to the norms that have been established for the LPI across a population of approximately ten thousand leaders and fifty thousand observers.

Reflection

After walking through the feedback, participants are given time to more thoroughly review all seven pages of their reports, analyze their results, and record their interpretations. There are usually anywhere from 250 to 500 different data points to review. This is an extraordinary amount of data to absorb, and it often takes hours to fully appreciate the meaning of the messages. Rather than try to absorb all of this in one sitting, we suggest participants return to the data at least five more times in a typical workshop—once for each practice.

In *The Leadership Challenge Workshop*™, we ask participants to share LPI scores with one other participant. The partner's role is to view the data from another perspective and to offer peer support for development. Because this information is sensitive, it is always the participant's decision whether to share scores.

Practice and Application

Feedback alone is of little benefit to the recipient unless it is followed by opportunities for goal setting, mastery, and confidence building. In *The Leadership Challenge Workshops*™ offered by The Tom Peters Group/Learning Systems, which last two or three days, participants experience each practice, observe what to do to perform it well, get opportunities to try out specific behaviors, receive additional feedback on their performance, apply their lessons to their own settings, and make commitments on how they will follow through.

Assessing Strategic Competencies Online

Stephen E. Forrer

Strategic development means linking individual development to the organization's long-term business goals. Conceptual Systems' Assessing Strategic Competencies (ASC Online) helps organizations do this. It is a comprehensive 360° tool that is online—delivery and set-up with the human resources (HR) department and administrators, questionnaire distribution to managers and users, feedback by raters, and processing and reporting to HR, managers, teams, and individuals. (See Exhibit A.2.)

ASC Online starts with the organization's or team's business challenges and required competencies. The HR administrator sets up the project using simple prompts that let the administrator define the people and the competencies to be assessed. Managers can then use that template to input specific skills for their teams to assess. The individual is able to receive feedback on those competencies and associated skills that will actually make a difference to the success of the team. Users can track their questionnaires, link their feedback directly to development plans, and get tips on using coaches and mentors to get more effective feedback. Raters receive online training on being a good rater, attach confidential comments, and save copies of their feedback. All of this is achieved electronically, giving a dependable level of speed and accuracy.

For Employees

The system sends a note to the user when all of the questionnaires have been returned and the data analyzed. In the Individual

Assessing Strategic Competencies™ product line has been developed by Conceptual Systems, Inc., 1010 Wayne Ave., Suite 1420, Silver Spring, MD 20910. For more information, call 301-589-1800. © 1996, Conceptual Systems, Inc.

Exhibit A.2. Assessing Strategic Competencies (ASC) Online

Development Profile Overview, the user sees a prioritized list of business challenges (when available), a prioritized list of competencies required to meet those challenges, and then a breakdown of his or her strengths, opportunities for continuous improvement, and development needs. The user can then access the three data reports—Report 1: Ratings on Competencies, in priority order; Report 2: Detailed Ratings on Skills Related to the Competencies, and Report 3: Competencies and Skills Most Important to Each Business Challenge.

Using these three reports and the overview, the user tries to answer the following questions:

- What strengths, if maintained, will allow me to make significant contributions in meeting future business challenges?

- For each competency I want to use to make contributions, are there specific skills that need to be developed?

- What competencies and skills provide the best opportunity for continuous improvement or development? (See Exhibit A.3.)

The system prompts the user to be strategic, to develop the competencies that match the critical needs of the team, business, or organization. The user takes the information displayed in the reports, together with the related development ideas that are shown, and creates an online Individual Development Plan. If additional ideas are needed to complete the plan, the user can access the online Development Resources Database of over five thousand generic ideas. The user forwards the completed plan to his or her manager as part of a development discussion.

The user is also prompted to utilize "development coaches" during the feedback process. The system prompts the user as well as the selected coach in techniques that improve the quality of the feedback and the resulting development plans.

Exhibit A.3. Sample Individual Development Profile Overview

ASC ONLINE: ASC Online Sample 3 (questionnaire)

File Edit View ASC Options Window Help

Your Results

Challenge 1: *Implement reengineering changes to increase productivity and reduce costs.*

Competencies and Related Skills	Development Need			Opportunity for Continuous Improvement		Strength to Maintain	
	1	2	3	4	5	6	7
Planning and Organizing						□●X	
Implementing						X●	
Developing People	●X						
Business Awareness				X□		●	
Personal Leadership				□X●			
Quality				X□●			
Analysis						●X	
Conflict Management	X●						
Team Facilitation			▣				
Decision Making			X□●				
Written Communication						●□X	
Negotiation						□X	
Oral Communication	●X						
Relationship Building				X□●			
Technical/Functional Expertise	□X						
Customer Service				X□●			

Scale		Raters
0-Not observed	4-Adequate Performance	**X** Self Score
1-Little or No Demonstrated Proficiency	5-Meets Expectations	● Manager's Score
2-Needs Significant Improvement	6-Exceeds Expectations	□ Other's Mean Score (4 raters)
3-Some Improvement Needed	7-Role Model	▨ Reference Group

For Managers

Managers can include specific skills or team challenges that they want their team members to assess. They can also approve the selection of raters. After the questionnaires are compiled, they receive an online Team Development Profile that they can analyze in a variety of ways. (See Exhibit A.4.) Reports might include:

- Mean scores by competency for each category of rater and the percentage of team members that fall into that category (Strength, Opportunity for Continuous Improvement, and Development Need)
- A Business Challenges Report that lists competencies that have been identified as being most important to the particular business challenges, broken into the three categories of Strength, Opportunity, or Development Need

Managers also receive a specific list of related development suggestions and access to the online Development Resources Database. They can use all this information to do online Team Development Planning, including the Planning Guide that details the process of creating a Team Development Plan.

Completion of the feedback process prior to a team meeting greatly improves the outcome of the team planning process. The feedback is also a sound foundation for individual development discussions.

For the Organization

The online HR ReportWriter gives all the aggregated data to the HR specialist to use for nearly unlimited analysis. Data can be analyzed by demographics, competency or skill, function, and so forth, to determine trends and needs for development. Since the software is fully customizable by the organization, this information can be extremely valuable in strategic HR planning. (See Exhibit A.5.)

Exhibit A.4. Sample Team Development Profile Overview

```
ASC ONLINE: ASC Online Sample 3 (questionnaire)          _ 🗗 ☒
File  Edit  View  ASC  Options  Window  Help
🖨 |◀ ◀ ▶ ▶| 🕐 📝 📰 🕮 | 📝 📇 🗂 ⬜
ASC Navigator                                            _ ☐ ☒
```

Your Results

Challenge 1: *Implement reengineering changes to increase productivity and reduce costs.*

Competencies and Related Skills	Development Need			Opportunity for Continuous Improvement		Strength to Maintain	
	1	2	3	4	5	6	7
Planning and Organizing						□●X	
Implementing							X●●
Developing People		●X					
Business Awareness				X□		●	
Personal Leadership				□X●			
Quality				X□●			
Analysis					X	●	
Conflict Management	X●						
Team Facilitation			●	X			
Decision Making			X●	□			
Written Communication						●	□X
Negotiation					□	X	
Oral Communication		□X●					
Relationship Building						□X	●
Technical/Functional Expertise		●□	X				
Customer Service					X□	●	

Scale		Raters
0-Not observed	4-Adequate Performance	**X** Self (10)
1-Little or No Demonstrated Proficiency	5-Meets Expectations	● Manager's Score (10)
2-Needs Significant Improvement	6-Exceeds Expectations	□ Other's Mean Score (37)
3-Some Improvement Needed	7-Role Model	▨ Reference Group

Exhibit A.5. Sample HR ReportWriter Data Report

HR ReportWriter

Exit Help

| Introduction | Demographics | Competencies | Business Challenges | Data Reports |

View Report

Zoom [75] ▶   Close

Page [1] of [1]

- Including all demographic responses

For the following population:
- XYZ Organization

Total Population | 65

This report displays the individuals in the population whose overall summary feedback rating fell into the categories shown. Summary scores are determined by calculating the average of all scores.

Competency	Development Need	Opportunity for Continuous Improvement	Strength to Maintain	Summary Rating	Mean	Low Score	High Score
Analysis	5 (7.7%)	55 (84.6%)	5 (7.7%)	0	4.74	1	7
Communication	2 (3.1%)	57 (87.7%)	6 (9.2%)	0	4.87	1	7
Customer Focus	3 (4.6%)	57 (87.7%)	5 (7.7%)	0	4.78	1	7

Main Menu   View Report   Print Report

Influence Style Questionnaire

Tom Rose
Situation Management Systems, Inc.

A prominent feature of any Situation Management System (SMS) competency development program is the use of assessment questionnaires that help participants clarify their strengths and development needs with respect to the targeted competency. These questionnaires assess performance in such areas as behavioral influence, negotiation, and project management. To illustrate the SMS approach, we will refer to the Influence Style Questionnaire (ISQ), a survey that is used in SMS's Positive Power and Influence Program (PPIP).

The ISQ helps participants collect focused feedback from others about their use of influence styles and behavior. Like other good 360° surveys, the ISQ has good psychometric properties. Research has demonstrated that individual items in the survey discriminate well, relate to the dimensions they are theorized to relate to, and so on.

A discussion of the three main differences that distinguish SMS's approach from common practice follows.

Who Completes the Questionnaires?

Pre-program instructions ask participants to distribute ISQ questionnaires to five people. Unlike many 360° tools, this one does not require that respondents include senior, peer, and junior colleagues. Participants are simply instructed to identify people whom it is important to influence. Often, however, we find that participants collect data from a 360° sweep of their work situation.

For more information about this assessment tool, please contact Tom Rose, Ph.D., 195 Hanover Street, Hanover, MA 02339.

Another departure from common 360° practice is that we recommend the distribution of questionnaires to fewer people than is typical. Firms administering 360° feedback surveys often require at least three to five responses from direct reports and peers so that sound statistical comparisons can be made between a particular participant's scores and norm group scores. Such statistical comparisons are not a feature of our feedback process, because we believe that skillful and effective influence is ideographic to specific people pursuing specific objectives. Generalizations drawn from comparisons of the average associate ratings with norm information are not likely to help a person plan how to improve a work relationship with a specific peer, with whom a particular work objective is being pursued.

The Anonymity of the Feedback

The ISQ feedback process is explicitly not anonymous. Respondents are asked to return the completed questionnaires directly to the participant. The participant reviews the completed ISQs and records the results on blank profile sheets we provide. We use a nonanonymous administration process, because the program is explicitly devoted to enhancing influence skills by focusing on current work relationships. Consequently, participants must know what results are associated with what respondent to establish an unambiguous baseline for these relationships.

We handle concerns about possible distortions in the data caused by the lack of anonymity in two ways. First, while acknowledging that individual ratings may be influenced by rater motivation, we explain that such distortion does not generally affect the relative pattern of high to low ratings—the ratings of greatest interpretive value. Second, when extreme responses occur (for example, a respondent gives all behaviors the highest or lowest possible ratings or refuses to complete the questionnaire), we help participants plan how they will engage with that respondent to begin building or restoring trust in the relationship.

How the Data Are Interpreted

A participant plots the results from completed questionnaires on the two types of blank profiles we provide in pre-program materials—one for self-ratings and one for ratings from associates. Participants bring these profiles and the completed questionnaires to the training program. Reviewing differences between self-ratings and associate ratings helps participants identify important differences between the intended and actual impact of their behavior. Exploring differences between intent and impact is a major theme of our Positive Power and Influence Program.

In Exhibit A.6, an example of a completed "Ratings by Associates" profile is shown.

During the program, participants examine responses to the individual items contained in the ISQ. Also during the program, consultants encourage participants to consider their results in light of possible adjustments in future influence practice. More specifically, we instruct participants to construe patterns in the data as explicit requests from respondents to do something differently (Do more of X. Do less of Y.) or as requests to maintain one's current practice (Stay the same.).

As participants work through the data, we help them identify major surprises, responses that are off the scale, and major differences between respondents. Themes of consistency and inconsistency are explored with different categories of respondents (that is, less productive relationships versus more productive relationships, senior colleagues versus junior colleagues, fellow employees versus customers, and so on).

Throughout the process, we coach participants to evaluate their specific scores in light of specific influence situations. A high score might mean someone is using a behavior more frequently than is appropriate, while a low score, rather than being negative, might indicate that the participant rarely encounters situations that require a certain style or behavior. A detailed situational analysis

Exhibit A.6. Influence Style Profile: Ratings by Associates (SMS)

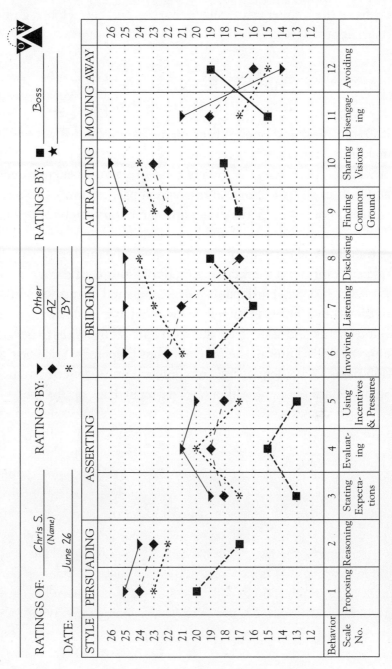

helps participants determine whether it is desirable to increase or decrease the frequency of influence styles and behaviors recorded on their profile.

How the Results Are Used in the PPIP Training Program

ISQ information is one of three major forms of assessment information that participants receive in a typical SMS program. The other assessment takes the form of a videotaped assessment exercise and "fish bowl" role plays, during which participants experiment with each of the influence styles and their component behaviors. These exercises are completed by mid-morning on the second day of training, and participants are then given the opportunity to distill key points from their various kinds of assessment data.

Once program participants have completed the assessment activities, they identify influence styles or behaviors they want to develop further and select from among a series of exercises to develop targeted skills. Later in the program, they prepare and rehearse action plans for implementing our approach to influence to achieve an important outcome with a work associate back on the job.

The PROFILOR Family

Susan Gebelein
and PDI's Profile Development Teams

The PROFILOR Family, the family of profiles from executive-level to individual contributor positions created by Personnel Decisions International (PDI), focuses on what PDI believes is the primary goal of multi-rater feedback—development. Each of PDI's profiles includes summary information identifying highest and lowest ratings and a focus for development.

The PDI profiles provide developmental recommendations for each behavior identified as a development need. These recommendations are for on-the-job action steps and stretch assignments and include books and seminars as development resources.

PDI also provides a computer-based development and coaching tool—DevelopMentor—which enables individuals using the PDI profiles to quickly complete a development plan and then concentrate on development and coaching activities designed to support the plan.

The examples provided (Exhibits A.7 through A.11, on the following pages) illustrate portions of the data received in the PROFILOR Feedback Report. The standard feedback report is both comprehensive and specific. It contains summary information, as illustrated in the exhibits that follow, as well as behavior or item-specific results. It should be noted that the Focus for Development section incorporates PDI normative data, as well as data from other sections of the report. The various presentations of the data are designed to assist the recipient in interpreting the report and greatly enhance development planning efforts.

For more information about this assessment tool, please contact Susan Gebelein at Personnel Decisions International, 2000 Plaza VII Tower, 45 South Seventh Street, Minneapolis, MN 55402.

Exhibit A.7. Highest Ratings (PROFILOR/PDI)

	Rating	Ratings by Others				Rank
	Self	Boss	Dir Rpt	Peer/Coll	Average	
Readily put in extra time and effort	4.00	5.00	5.00	5.00	5.00	1
Apply accurate logic in solving problems	5.00	5.00	4.75	4.67	4.81	2
Coordinate work with other groups	4.00	4.00	5.00	5.00	4.67	3
Are accessible to provide assistance/support as necessary	3.00	4.00	5.00	5.00	4.67	4
Understand complex concepts and relationships	5.00	4.00	5.00	4.67	4.56	5
Analyze problems from different points of view	5.00	4.00	4.75	4.67	4.47	6
Learn new information quickly	5.00	4.00	4.75	4.67	4.47	7
Focus on important information without getting bogged down in unnecessary detail	5.00	4.00	4.50	4.67	4.39	8
Seek out new work challenges	5.00	4.00	5.00	4.00	4.33	9
Set high personal standards of performance	4.00	4.00	4.00	5.00	4.33	10
Persist in the face of obstacles	4.00	4.00	5.00	4.00	4.33	11
Put top priority on getting results	5.00	3.00	5.00	5.00	4.33	12
Give people the latitude to manage their own responsibilities	4.00	4.00	4.00	5.00	4.33	13
Integrate planning efforts across work units	3.00	4.00	5.00	4.00	4.33	14
Anticipate problems and develop contingency plans	4.00	4.00	5.00	4.00	4.33	15
Make sound decisions based on adequate information	4.00	5.00	3.50	4.00	4.17	16
Make timely decisions	4.00	5.00	3.50	4.00	4.17	17
Initiate activities without being asked to do so	3.00	4.00	4.00	4.00	4.00	18
Display a high energy level	4.00	4.00	4.00	4.00	4.00	19
Convey a sense of urgency when appropriate	5.00	3.00	4.00	5.00	4.00	20

Exhibit A.8. Lowest Ratings (PROFILOR/PDI)

	Rating	Ratings by Others				Rank
	Self	Boss	Dir Rpt	Peer/Coll	Average	
Let people know when results are not up to expectations	4.00	2.00	1.00	2.00	1.67	1
Coach others in the development of their skills	4.00	2.00	2.00	1.00	1.67	2
Show interest in employees' careers	4.00	2.00	2.00	1.00	1.67	3
Take a stand and resolve important issues	5.00	2.00	2.00	2.00	2.00	4
Drive hard on the right issues	5.00	2.00	2.00	2.00	2.00	5
Act decisively	4.00	2.00	2.00	2.00	2.00	6
Involve others in shaping plans and decisions that affect them	3.00	2.00	2.00	2.00	2.00	7
Provide challenging assignments to facilitate individual development	4.00	2.00	2.00	2.00	2.00	8
Know when to supervise and coach people and when to leave them on their own	4.00	2.00	2.00	2.00	2.00	9
Value the contributions of all team members	4.00	2.00	2.00	3.00	2.33	10
Give specific and constructive feedback	4.00	3.00	1.00	3.00	2.33	11
Get others to take action	4.00	3.00	2.25	2.33	2.53	12
Inspire people to excel	4.00	3.00	2.25	2.33	2.53	13
Reward people for good performance	4.00	3.00	2.50	2.33	2.61	14
Confront problems early, before they get out of hand	4.00	3.00	2.00	3.00	2.67	15
Challenge others to make tough choices	4.00	3.00	2.00	3.00	2.67	16
Are assertive	4.00	3.00	3.00	2.00	2.67	17
Use a team approach to solve problems when appropriate	3.00	3.00	2.00	3.00	2.67	18
Foster teamwork within the team	3.00	3.00	3.00	2.00	2.67	19
Promote teamwork among groups; discourage "we vs. they" thinking	3.00	3.00	3.00	2.00	2.67	20

Exhibit A.9. Focus for Development:
Building on Key Strengths (PROFILOR/PDI)

Name

General Strengths	Behaviors
Analyze Issues	Apply accurate logic in solving problems
	Analyze problems from different points of view
Manage Execution	Coordinate work with other groups
	Are accessible to provide assistance/support as necessary
Show Work Commitment	Readily put in extra time and effort
	Seek out new work challenges

Note: The above three skills were rated highest by "others" relative to the norm group.

Boss Perspective	Self Perspective

Manage Disagreements
  Facilitate the discussion and resolution of different views
	Show Work Commitment
	  Readily put in extra time and effort

Work toward win/win solutions whenever possible	Seek out new work challenges

Use Sound Judgment
  Make timely decisions
	Drive for Results
	  Persist in the face of obstacles

Make sound decisions based on adequate information	Put top priority on getting results

Analyze Issues
  Apply accurate logic in solving problems
	Use Sound Judgment
	  Make timely decisions

Analyze problems from different points of view	Make sound decisions based on adequate information
Note: Skills rated most important by "boss" and highest in skill by "others" relative to the norm group.	Note: Skills rated most important by "self" and highest in skill by "others" relative to the norm group.

Exhibit A.10. Focus for Development:
Addressing Development Needs (PROFILOR/PDI)

Name

General Development Needs	Behaviors
Coach and Develop	Let people know when results are not up to expectations
	Show interest in employees' careers
Lead Courageously	Drive hard on the right issues
	Act decisively
Foster Teamwork	Involve others in shaping plans and decisions that affect them
	Value the contributions of all team members

Note: The above three skills were rated lowest by "others" relative to the norm group.

Boss Perspective	Self Perspective
Coach and Develop	Act with Integrity
Let people know when results are not up to expectations	Protect confidential information
Show interest in employees' careers	Show consistency between words and actions
Lead Courageously	Provide Direction
Drive hard on the right issues	Link the team's mission to that of the broader organization
Act decisively	Make the team mission and strategies clear to others
Foster Teamwork	Influence Others
Involve others in shaping plans and decisions that affect them	Get others to take action
Value the contributions of all team members	Negotiate persuasively

Note: Skills rated most important by "boss" and highest in skill by "others" relative to the norm group.	Note: Skills rated most important by "self" and highest in skill by "others" relative to the norm group.

Exhibit A.11. Development Suggestion:
Foster Teamwork (PROFILOR/PDI)

Developmental Objective: Involve others in shaping plans and decisions
that affect them

On-the-Job Activities

People who assist in the planning and decision making are likely to be
more invested in the successful execution of those plans and decisions.
Engage all your team members in the development of your team's mission, strategy, and goals. When working on projects involving other
functions, include representatives from all affected areas. Following is
a technique for involving others:

1. Identify everyone who should be involved. Check with others to be
   sure that you haven't missed anyone.

2. Meet with these people and give them the big picture of what is
   happening. Ask for the help you want from them. Clarity about
   your purpose is important. You may want to:

   • Simply inform people about the plan.

   • Show how your plan will affect them.

   • Get help in identifying the problem or opportunity.

   • Have them determine a course of action.

3. Conduct the meeting so that you get the input you need and the
   team feels involved in the process. Develop a plan to keep the team
   informed.

With the team members' mutual investment in the objective, you will
be better able to get others to buy into your goal.

Recommended Readings

Katzenbach, J. R., and Smith, D. K. *The Wisdom of Teams*. Boston:
Harvard Business School Press, 1993. ISBN: 0–87584–367–0.

Parker, Glenn M. *Team Players and Teamwork*. San Francisco: Jossey-
Bass, 1990. ISBN: 1–55542–257–8.

Suggested Seminar

Facilitative Leadership: Tapping the Power of Participation.
Interaction Associates, Inc., 600 Townsend Street, Suite 550,
San Francisco, CA 94103, 415/241–8000.

VOICES®: Electronic Feedback System

Michael M. Lombardo and Robert W. Eichinger

VOICES® is a PC-based, 360°-plus feedback system. Due to the flexibility of electronic systems:

Users can determine the input. They can use the CAREER ARCHITECT® competencies loaded into the system or add their own.

They can give feedback on many competencies or a few.

Users determine the output. Using a spreadsheet, they can construct up to six-column feedback summaries for any data available.

Users can select from about thirty standard reports loaded into the program or modify and save them.

Nineteen relationship cuts are available. Along with the usual self, boss, direct reports, and peers, there are many others such as customers, past associates, human resource professionals, mentors, out-of-unit peers, indirect reports, boss's boss, even spouse.

Optional demographics include gender, how long raters have known the person, how often they have worked with the person, citizenship, and race or ethnic group.

For more information about this assessment tool, please contact Michael M. Lombardo or Robert W. Eichinger at Lominger Limited, Inc., 1825 Girard Avenue South, Minneapolis, MN 55403.

Raters get feedback while they are rating, so they can see how their ratings are distributed.

Raters set their own level of confidentiality. They decide whether their ratings are open (available in a group of one), in a group of two, or restricted to a group of three or more.

Raters can add notes at any time—competency-specific ones or more general comments.

Additionally, VOICES® uses a rating scale that is different from most instruments. Among the items: Is this a towering strength for the person? Is the person talented, skilled, weak? Is this a serious issue for the person? Since the intent is confidential feedback for development, it does the learner no good to receive all high scores (or low ones), so the instructions ask raters to spread their ratings and try to think in relative terms—to consider what developmental messages they want to send.

The VOICES® Administrator Program maintains the database for access to unlimited group reports, which may be cut however the organization sets them up—by performance or potential, by function, department, strategic business unit, and so forth.

The VOICES® Process

Specifically:

1. The administrator prepares feedback disks by selecting which competencies and questions are to be rated and may add special company- or job-specific competencies.

2. The disks are sent to raters, who complete them at their own PCs and return them to the administrator.

3. A report disk is created by the Administrator Program and forwarded to the VOICES® facilitator, who conducts the feedback with the learner.

Feedback with VOICES®

Some organizations create a series of reports that are printed for all learners. Others leave this to the discretion of the feedback facilitator.

The facilitator then prepares for the session, usually by starting with basic reports like overall competency and importance ratings and building toward more complex analyses (see Exhibit A.12).

The goal of VOICES® is in-depth analysis (although it can be used for basic feedback by deleting many of the questions and competencies). The VOICES® questions include ratings of competence and questions about (1) whether the person overuses the competency (if present), (2) importance of the competency, (3) sureness of the rater, (4) whether the person has changed on the competency in the past year, and (5) how the rater thinks the learner would rate himself or herself on this competency. Using this information, the facilitator can have an in-depth discussion with the learner, not simply look at a single competency or importance rating.

Sample issues that often come up include:

"I don't understand how people can even rate that. They've never seen me do this." The facilitator can check the ratings for sureness.

"I wonder how they thought I'd rate myself." The facilitator can say, for example, "They thought you'd rate yourself higher than you actually did."

"I think people who used to work with me wouldn't say that." The facilitator can check what past associates said.

"I wonder if men and women would agree on that." The facilitator can check the gender data.

"This is my greatest strength." Using the question about overuse, the facilitator can see if the person does too much of it, as well as whether it is having some negative consequences.

A.12. Selected Demographics (VOICES®)

Printed For:
Business Unit:

Item	Skill Rating 7 / Average Worked Once / Scale: 1–5	Skill Rating 5 / Average More Than Once / Scale: 1–5	Skill Rating 6 / Average Male / Scale: 1–5	Skill Rating 5 / Average Female / Scale: 1–5	Skill Rating 4 / Average 31–39 / Scale 1–5	Skill Rating 5 / Average 40–49 / Scale 1–5
Vision						
58 Strategic Agility	4.33	4.80	4.40	4.60	4.50	4.60
2 Dealing with Ambiguity	4.00	4.40	3.87	4.60	4.75	4.00
65 Managing Vision and Purpose	3.86	4.80	4.17	4.20	4.00	4.40
14 Creativity	3.83	4.00	3.80	4.00	3.75	4.00
28 Innovation Management	3.83	4.00	4.20	4.00	3.75	4.40
46 Perspective	3.83	4.20	4.00	4.00	3.75	4.20
17 Decision Quality	3.80	3.60	3.75	3.60	3.50	3.75
32 Learning on the Fly	3.67	3.75	3.40	4.00	4.00	3.60
51 Problem Solving	3.67	3.80	3.60	3.80	3.75	3.60
40 Dealing with Paradox	3.17	4.00	3.60	3.40	3.50	3.40
Vision Overall:	3.80	4.14	3.86	4.02	3.93	4.00
Knowledgeability						
24 Functional/Technical Skills	4.60	3.80	3.75	4.40	4.75	3.50
30 Intellectual Horsepower	4.43	4.40	4.17	4.80	4.75	4.40
49 Presentation Skills	3.88	4.20	3.33	4.80	4.75	3.40
5 Business Acumen	3.88	3.80	3.50	4.20	4.25	3.40
46 Perspective	3.83	4.20	4.00	4.00	3.75	4.20
67 Written Communications	3.71	3.80	3.83	3.60	3.50	3.80
61 Technical Learning	3.33	3.50	3.20	3.60	3.75	3.20
27 Informing	3.00	2.80	2.60	3.40	3.50	2.60

Exhibit A.13. Leadership Architect®
Portrait Writer™ Report

Printed For:
    Unit:
    High: 2, 5, 8, 9, 14, 18, 24, 25, 28, 29, 30, 34, 38, 46, 49, 50, 51, 56, 57, 58, 63, 65, 67
    Low: 3, 7, 10, 12, 13, 15, 20, 27, 31, 33, 35, 37, 41, 42, 44, 45, 47, 48, 54, 55, 59, 64
    Content: Effective Behaviors

Percent Match	Behavior
100 percent	

Listened to by higher management on business/strategy issues
Knows substance backing up vision
Can see likely futures
Strong champion of new ideas
Courage to present the unvarnished truth
Work designs/redesigns last longer than most
Knows where to look for answers in the organization
Innovates in the broader strategic context
Can create his/her own innovative ideas
Balances future perspective with here and now
Always in tune with thinking about the new and different
Can write good mission/vision/values statements
Goes where the talent is even outside the organization
Seeks broad counsel/sources in problem solving
Has courage to present controversial subjects

Content: Ineffective Behaviors

Percent Match	Behavior
100 percent	

Has many good ideas but doesn't share them comfortably with others
Lack of self insight may chill good hiring decisions for people reporting to him/her
Doesn't do much to personally improve
Won't accept help/input on writing
Understands how organizations work but doesn't have the skills to take advantage of the knowledge
Impatient with those who don't understand or support the vision

(continued)

Exhibit A.13. Leadership Architect®
Portrait Writer™ Report, Cont'd.

Percent Match	Behavior
	Criticism delivered with a hammer
	Doesn't line up allies—candid loner
	Doesn't relate well to those less intelligent
	Not very people-oriented
	Won't take any counsel—goes ahead and says what he/she thinks
	Isn't as good communicating the vision in small groups

Generally, facilitators follow a build-up strategy—start with basic reports and have more detailed reports for back-up as questions arise. The goal is to get to a few developmental needs by looking at the results many different ways. Facilitators often close with a summary of likely strengths and weaknesses using PORTRAIT WRITER™ (see Exhibit A.13)—a feature of VOICES®. This gets the person away from thinking in numbers and presents some narrative statements that may characterize the person.

Checklist for Selecting a Questionnaire

Exhibit B.1. Checklist for Selecting a Questionnaire: Screening Criteria

The Initial Search	Alternatives						
Screening Criteria	A	B	C	D	E	F	G
A complete set of sample materials has been requested and received.							
The theoretical model that the questionnaire is based on is consistent with the organization's needs and values.							
Face validity has been confirmed by representatives of the target population and key stakeholders.							
The instrument provides good value for the price.							
Remaining alternatives?							

The initial search is made up of *Screening Criteria*. Each alternative is rated a "go" or a "no go." Only the alternatives that meet all screening criteria should be given further consideration.

The remaining alternatives should be evaluated against the *Comparing Criteria*—the alternative that meets the most comparing criteria the best will be the preferred choice.

Exhibit B.2. Checklist for Selecting a Questionnaire: Comparing Criteria

The In-depth Evaluation	Alternatives		
Comparing Criteria	A	B	C
The Questionnaire			

What research has been conducted on the questionnaire?
   Test-retest consistency (.5)
   Internal consistency (.65 to .85)
   Inter-rater agreement (.5)
   What were the results of the validity study showing a relationship between the items measured and effectiveness on the job?			

How are the questions structured?
   Behavioral
   Positive
   Personal
   Multidimensional			

The Feedback Report			

What features does the feedback report have, and which best meet your needs?
   Length of the report
   Safeguards confidentiality
   Provides importance ratings
   Shows feedback from different perspectives
   Compares self and other ratings
   Compares ratings to a norm
   Displays items as well as scales
   Includes recommendations
   Has open-ended questions			

(continued)

Exhibit B.2. Checklist for Selecting a Questionnaire: Comparing Criteria, Cont'd.

The In-depth Evaluation	Alternatives		
Comparing Criteria	A	B	C
The Support Materials			
For the feedback recipients: To what extent do the materials explain how to interpret and make the most of the data? To what extent do the materials assist the recipient to identify key areas for development and to plan for next steps?			
For the trainer or facilitator: How complete and useful are the guidelines for administering the feedback process? How complete and useful are the guidelines as aids to the trainer in helping the recipient interpret the report? How clear are the scoring methods and their implications?			

Sample Worksheets for Feedback Analysis and Interpretation

Exhibit C.1. Consolidation of Feedback

Summarize your key strengths, weaknesses, and areas for clarification
on the chart.

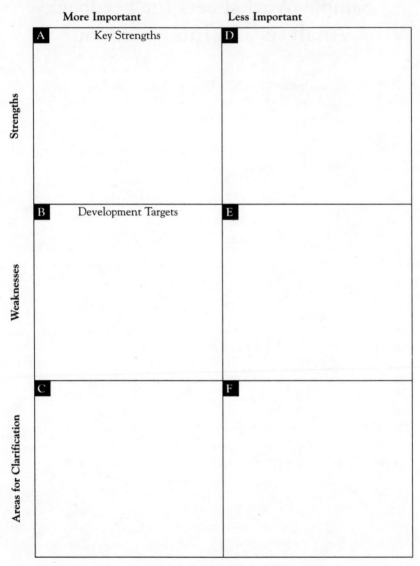

Key Strengths

Using the key strengths you've identified in Box A of the previous page, answer these questions:

1. In what kinds of situations does this strength serve you well?

2. In what situations might this strength be less useful?

3. What steps could you take to leverage these strengths?

Key Development Target

- Why is it important to do this differently? How will it help me be more effective (or successful, or satisfied with my job)?

- What gets in the way of my doing it?

- How might I overcome these barriers?

- How can I use my strengths to help me?

- How can I minimize my risk when starting a new practice or behavior?

Areas for Clarification

1. Feedback that I find confusing, incomplete, or contradictory:

2. Who could help me understand this better?

3. When will I meet with them?

Development Goal

Area for Development:

1. Developmental Goal:

2. Criteria for Success:

3a. Typical Strategy: b. Actions/Next Steps:

4a. Additional Strategies: b. Actions/Next Steps:

Sharing and Clarifying Feedback

When you return to the job, it's important to share and clarify the feedback you have gotten from your colleagues, direct reports, and boss(es). If possible, call a separate meeting with each group. Here are some suggested action steps to follow during the meeting:

- *Express appreciation.* Thank the group for providing anonymous feedback, and describe how the feedback was useful.

- *Give an overview.* Provide a summary of your strengths and development targets as perceived by the group.

- *Ask for input.* Ask for the group's input on the areas you have identified, and then offer your ideas.

- *Discuss issues for clarification.* Ask the group to help you understand feedback you found surprising or confusing.

- *Summarize next steps.* Commit to actions you will take based on the feedback, and ask for people's help if appropriate.

- *Ask for ongoing feedback.* Invite the group to let you know how you are doing, and set a follow-up date.

Sharing and Clarifying Feedback

Skill Practice
Meeting Notes

Which group are you meeting with (colleagues, direct reports, bosses)? What will you say?

1. Thank the group for feedback, and describe how it was useful.

2. Summary of *strengths* as seen by the group (refer to pages 60 and 61 in feedback report).

   Development targets as seen by the group.

3. Ask for input.

   Notes on group's ideas and suggestions:
   (complete during meeting)

   Offer your ideas.

4. Outline *issues for clarification* and ask for input.

   Notes on suggestions/clarifications:
   (complete during meeting)

5. Summarize actions you will take based on feedback.
   (complete during meeting)

6. Ask for ongoing feedback and set a follow-up date.

Next Steps

- Sharing and Clarifying meetings

  with _____

  by _____ .

  (date)

- Complete Planning Guide

  by _____ .

  (date)

- Initial actions to be taken to leverage strengths:

- Initial actions to be taken to address weaknesses:

- Other:

360° Feedback Administration Flowchart

Exhibit D.1. Questionnaire Administration Process

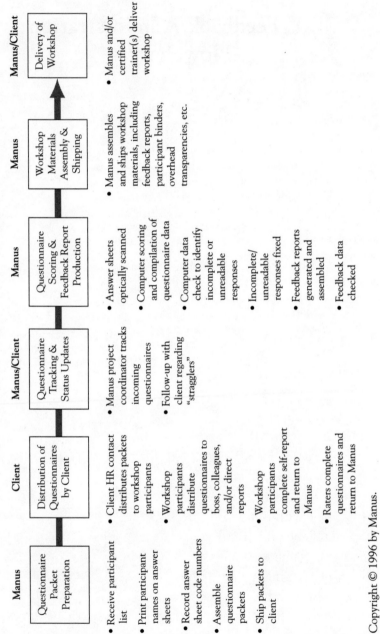

Manus	Client	Manus/Client	Manus	Manus	Manus/Client
Questionnaire Packet Preparation	Distribution of Questionnaires by Client	Questionnaire Tracking & Status Updates	Questionnaire Scoring & Feedback Report Production	Workshop Materials Assembly & Shipping	Delivery of Workshop

Questionnaire Packet Preparation
- Receive participant list
- Print participant names on answer sheets
- Record answer sheet code numbers
- Assemble questionnaire packets
- Ship packets to client

Distribution of Questionnaires by Client
- Client HR contact distributes packets to workshop participants
- Workshop participants distribute questionnaires to boss, colleagues, and/or direct reports
- Workshop participants complete self-report and return to Manus
- Raters complete questionnaires and return to Manus

Questionnaire Tracking & Status Updates
- Manus project coordinator tracks incoming questionnaires
- Follow-up with client regarding "stragglers"

Questionnaire Scoring & Feedback Report Production
- Answer sheets optically scanned
- Computer scoring and compilation of questionnaire data
- Computer data check to identify incomplete or unreadable responses
- Incomplete/unreadable responses fixed
- Feedback reports generated and assembled
- Feedback data checked

Workshop Materials Assembly & Shipping
- Manus assembles and ships workshop materials, including feedback reports, participant binders, overhead transparencies, etc.

Delivery of Workshop
- Manus and/or certified trainer(s) deliver workshop

Notes

Chapter One

1. O'Reilly, B. "360 [Degree] Feedback Can Change Your Life." *Fortune*, October 17, 1994, 93–97.
2. Bongiorno, L. "How'm I Doing? This Creative Management Program Uses Tough Love." *Business Week*, October 23, 1995, 72–74.
3. London, M., and Smithers, J. W. "Can Multi-source Feedback Change Perceptions of Goal Accomplishment, Self-Evaluations and Performance Related to Outcomes? Theory-Based Applications and Directions for Research." SUNY at Stony Brook and La Salle University, 1995. Paper accepted for publication in *Personnel Psychology*.
4. McCall, M. W., Jr., Lombardo, M. M., and Morrison, A. M. *The Lessons of Experience: How Successful Executives Develop on the Job*. Lexington, Mass.: Lexington Books, 1988.
5. Lindsey, E. H., Homes, V., and McCall, M. W., Jr. *Key Events in Executives' Lives*, Technical Report #32. Greensboro, N.C.: The Center for Creative Leadership, 1987.
6. Interview with Randall White, November 1995.
7. Special Issue on 360-degree Feedback. *Human Resource Management*, Summer/Fall, *32*, 1993.
8. Interview with Margaret Van Voast, November 1995.
9. Interview with Rich Lupi, November 1995.
10. Interview, Lupi, 1995.
11. Interview with Margaret Van Voast, November 1995.
12. Interview, Van Voast, 1995.

13. Interview with Diane Frimmel, May 1996.
14. Interview with David DeVries, November 1995.
15. Interview with Randall White, November 1995.
16. Interview with Marion Jacobson, May 1996.
17. Interview with Steven Gonabe, May 1996.
18. London, M., and Smithers, J. W. "Can Multi-source Feedback Change Perceptions of Goal Accomplishment, Self-Evaluations and Performance Related to Outcomes? Theory-Based Applications and Directions for Research." SUNY at Stony Brook and La Salle University, 1995. Paper accepted for publication in *Personnel Psychology*.
19. Bracken, D. W. "Straight Talk About Multi-rater Feedback." *Training and Development*, September 1994, 44–51.
20. Timmreck, C. W. "Upward Feedback in the Trenches: Challenges and Realities." Paper presented at the tenth annual conference of the Society for Industrial and Organizational Psychology, Orlando, Fla., 1995.
21. Bernardin, H. J., and Beatty, R. W. "Can Subordinate Appraisal Enhance Leader Effectiveness?" *Sloan Management Review*, Summer 1987, 28(4), 63–73.

Chapter Two

1. Interview with Gail Howard, November 1995.
2. Interview, Howard, 1995.
3. Interview, Howard, 1995.
4. Interview, Howard, 1995.
5. Discussions with Dan Slocum, January–September 1994.
6. The Landmark Stock Exchange and the names of its employees are fictitious but based on a real case study.
7. Wright, G. "CM Firm Emphasizes Proactive Relationship with Owners." *Building Design and Construction*, February 1991, 58–60.
8. Wright, *Building Design and Construction*, 1991.
9. Interview with Rich Lupi, November 1995.
10. Interview, Lupi, 1995.
11. Interview, Lupi, 1995.

12. Interview with Margaret Van Voast, November 1995.
13. Interview with Rich Lupi, November 1995.
14. Interview with Allyn Keiser, June 1996.
15. Interview, Keiser, 1996.
16. Discussions with Joseph Schmidt, July–August 1994.
17. Interview with Gail Howard, November 1995.
18. Interview with Gail Howard, November 1995.
19. Discussions with Joseph Schmidt, July–August 1994.
20. Interview with Mary Clare Healy, May 1996.
21. Discussions with Joseph Schmidt, July–August 1994.
22. Interview with Ed Wiseman, February 1996.
23. Interview with Mary Clare Healy, May 1996.
24. Interview with Rich Lupi, November 1995.
25. Interview with Gary Zambardino, November 1995.
26. Interview with Gail Howard, November 1995.
27. Discussions with David Georgenson, January–December 1994.
28. Interview with Margaret Van Voast, November 1995.
29. Interview with Gary Zambardino, November 1995.
30. Interview with Rich Lupi, November 1995.
31. Interview with Gail Howard, November 1995.

Chapter Three

1. Morrison, A. M., McCall, M. W., Jr., and DeVries, D. L. *Feedback to Managers: A Comprehensive Review of Twenty-four Instruments.* Technical Report #8. Greensboro, N.C.: The Center for Creative Leadership, 1978.
2. Interview with senior manager (name withheld), September 1995.
3. Van Velsor, E., and Leslie, J. B. *Feedback to Managers Volume I: A Guide to Evaluating Multi-source Feedback Instruments.* Greensboro, N.C.: The Center for Creative Leadership, 1991.
4. Most of these volumes can be found in the reference section of the library: (1) *Feedback to Managers Volume II: A Review and Comparison of Sixteen Multi-rater Feedback Instruments* (E. Van Velsor, 1991, 1997), (2) *A Comprehensive Reference for Assessment*

in Psychology, Education, and Business (Sweetland and Keyser, 1986, 1990), (3) *Psychware Sourcebook* (King, 1987, 1988), (4) *Mental Measurement Yearbook* (Conoley and Kramer, 1989; Mitchell, 1985), (5) *The Directory of Human Resource Development Instrumentation* (Peters, 1985).

5. Yukl, G., Wall, S. J., and Lepsinger, R. "Preliminary Report on Validation of The Managerial Practices Survey." In K. E. Clark and M. B. Clark (ed.), *Measures of Leadership*. West Orange, N.J.: Leadership Library of America, 1990.

6. Van Velsor, E., and Wall, S. J. "How to Choose a Feedback Instrument." *Training Magazine*, March 1992, 48–51.

7. Van Velsor and Wall, *Training Magazine*, 1992.

8. Van Velsor, E., and Leslie, J. B. *Feedback to Managers Volume I: A Guide to Evaluating Multi-source Feedback Instruments*. Greensboro N.C.: The Center for Creative Leadership, 1991.

9. Yukl, G., and Lepsinger, R. "How To Get the Most Out of 360-degree Feedback." *Training Magazine*, December 1995, 45–50.

10. Yukl, G., and Manus Associates. *Compass: The Managerial Practices Survey Feedback Report*. Copyright 1996.

11. Van Velsor, E., and Wall, S. J. "How to Choose a Feedback Instrument." *Training Magazine*, March 1992, 48–51.

Chapter Four

1. Interview with David DeVries, November 1995.

2. Kaplan, R. E., and Palus, C. J. *Enhancing 360-degree Feedback for Senior Executives: How to Maximize the Benefit and Minimize the Risk*. Technical Report #160. Greensboro, N.C.: The Center for Creative Leadership, 1994.

3. Interview with Penny Nieroth, May 1996.

4. Interview with David DeVries, November 1995.

5. Interview, DeVries, 1995.

6. Interview, DeVries, 1995.

7. Kaplan, R. E., and Palus, C. J. *Enhancing 360-degree Feedback for Senior Executives: How to Maximize the Benefit and Minimize the*

Risk. Technical Report #160. Greensboro, N.C.: The Center for Creative Leadership, 1994.

8. Interview with David DeVries, November 1995.
9. Interview with Penny Nieroth, May 1996.
10. Interview with Harold Scharlatt, May 1996.

Chapter Five

1. Interview with Jay Strunk, November 1995.
2. We would like to thank Dave Berlew, who first introduced us to the Stakeholder Map.

Chapter Six

1. Ilgen, D. R., Fisher, C. D., and Taylor, M. S. "Consequences of Individual Feedback on Behavior in Organizations." *Journal of Applied Psychology,* 1979, 64(4), 349–371.
2. Milliman, J. F., and others. "Companies Evaluate Employees From All Perspectives." *Personnel Journal,* November 1994, 99–103.
3. Kaplan, R. E., and Palus, C. J. *Enhancing 360-degree Feedback for Senior Executives: How to Maximize the Benefit and Minimize the Risk.* Technical Report #160. Greensboro, N.C.: The Center for Creative Leadership, 1994.
4. Milliman, J. F., and others. "Companies Evaluate Employees From All Perspectives." *Personnel Journal,* November 1994, 99–103.

Chapter Seven

1. Interview with Harold Scharlatt, May 1996.
2. Interview with John Hoffman, May 1996.
3. Kaplan, R. E., Drath, W. H., and Kofodomos, J. R. *Beyond Ambition.* San Francisco: Jossey Bass, 1991, 200–225.
4. Kaplan, Drath, and Kofodomos, *Beyond Ambition,* 200–225.
5. Interview with John Hoffman, May 1996.
6. Interview with Penny Nieroth, May 1996.

7. Interview with Laura Daley-Caravella, May 1996.
8. Interview with Penny Nieroth, May 1996.
9. Interview with Laura Daley-Caravella, May 1996.
10. Yukl, G., and Lepsinger, R. "How To Get the Most Out of 360-degree Feedback." *Training Magazine*, December 1995, 45–50.
11. Yukl, G., and Manus Associates. *Compass: The Managerial Practices Survey Feedback Report*. Copyright 1996.
12. Yukl and Manus, *Compass*, 1996.
13. Yukl and Manus, *Compass*, 1996.

Chapter Eight

1. Yukl, G., and Manus Associates. *Compass: The Managerial Practices Survey Feedback Report*. Copyright 1996.
2. Interview with David DeVries, November 1995.
3. Yukl, G., and Manus Associates. *Compass: The Managerial Practices Survey Feedback Report*. Copyright 1996.
4. "Developmental Reference Points for Managers." *Benchmarks®️ Developmental Learning Guide*. Greensboro, N.C.: The Center for Creative Leadership.
5. Yukl, G., and Manus Associates. *Compass: The Managerial Practices Survey Feedback Report*. Copyright 1996.
6. McCall, M. W., Jr., Lombardo, M. M., and Morrison, A. M. *The Lessons of Experience: How Successful Executives Develop on the Job*. Lexington, Mass.: Lexington Books, 1988.
7. Yukl, G., and Manus Associates. *Compass: The Managerial Practices Survey Feedback Report*. Copyright 1996.

Chapter Nine

1. Ilgen, D. R., Fisher, C. D., and Taylor, M. S. "Consequences of Individual Feedback on Behavior in Organizations." *Journal of Applied Psychology*, 1979, 64(4), 349–371.
2. Interview with Jay Strunk, November 1995.
3. Interview, Strunk, 1995.
4. Edwards, M. R., and Ewen, A. J. *Multi-Source, 360-Degree Feedback Survey Results*. TEAMS, 1995.

5. Interview with Maxine Dalton, July 1996.
6. Timmerick, C. W., and Bracken, D. W. "Multisource Feedback Assessment: Reinforcing the Preferred 'Means' to the End." Paper presented at the eleventh annual conference of the Society of Industrial and Organizational Psychology, San Diego, April 1996.
7. Letter from Gary Yukl, June 1996.
8. Cronshaw, S. F., and Ford, R. G. "Effects of Categorization, Attribution, and Encoding Processes on Leadership Perceptions." *Journal of Applied Psychology*, 1987, *72*, 19.
9. DeNisi, A. S., Cafferty, T. P., and Meglino, B. M. "A Cognitive View of the Performance Appraisal Process: A Model and Research Proposition." *Organization Behavior and Human Performance*, 1984, *33*, 360–396.
10. DeNisi, Cafferty, and Meglino, *Organization Behavior and Human Performance*, 1984.
11. Campbell, D. J., and Lee, C. "Self-Appraisal in Performance Evaluation: Development Versus Evaluation." *Academy of Management Review*, 1988, *13*, 302–314.
12. Campbell and Lee, *Academy of Management Review*, 1988.
13. Edwards, M. R., and Ewen, A. J., "Moving Multisource Assessment Beyond Development. The linkage between 360–degree feedback, performance, and pay." *ACA Journal*, Winter 1995, 2–13.
14. Edwards and Ewen, *ACA Journal*, 1995.
15. Budman, M., and Rice, B. "The Rating Game." *Across the Board*, February 1994, 35–38.

Index